AF574185

RIVER FERRIES

OTHER BOOKS BY NANCY MARTIN — A SELECTION

Non-Fiction

Sea and River Pilots (Terence Dalton).
The Post Office — From Carrier Pigeon to Confravision (Dents).
The Fire Service Today (Dents).
Search and Rescue — The Story of the Coastguard Service (David & Charles).

School Books

Finn the Fisherboy (Macmillan).
Three Horses (Macmillan).
Three Dogs (Macmillan).
Three at the Zoo(Macmillan).

Career Books

Teresa joins the Red Cross (Macmillan).
Call the Nurse (Macmillan).
Four Girls in a Store (Macmillan).

Biography

William Carey — The Man who Never Gave Up (Hodder & Stoughton).

Anthology

Prayers for Children and Young People (Hodder & Stoughton).

RIVER FERRIES

by

NANCY MARTIN

TERENCE DALTON LIMITED
LAVENHAM . SUFFOLK
1980

Published by

TERENCE DALTON LIMITED

ISBN 0 900963 99 9

Text photoset in 11/12pt. Baskerville

Printed in Great Britain at
THE LAVENHAM PRESS LIMITED
LAVENHAM . SUFFOLK

Contents

Index of Illustrations

Acknowledgements

This book could not have been written but for the courtesy and co-operation of the many ferry authorities, their local managers, officers and crew. The same applies to the ferrymen on the smaller ferries and the retired ferrymen whom I met.

To all of these I offer my thanks and appreciation of the time they so willingly spent in providing me with information about their particular area of operation, and for their unfailing courtesy.

To single out any for special mention would be invidious, but I especially want to thank the ferry authorities who have kindly checked the parts of the manuscript which relate to their area, and the staff of many libraries around the country who gave me access to much information kept in their local studies sections.

I was not able to visit those ferries in the northern part of Scotland, but a journalist friend, Joan Alison, provided me with a great deal of information concerning the ferries in that area as a result of her own research.

To all of these, and to those who have kindly loaned photographs for reproduction in the book, I offer my sincere thanks. The photographs are acknowledged individually as and where they occur.

I have quoted from the work of others where it seemed right to do so and have acknowledged the source of the information used. If, quite unwittingly, I have failed to clear any copyright material used in this book, I apologise and due acknowledgement will be made in any future editions.

Nancy Martin
Fittleworth
1980

Preface

RIVER ferries have existed since man first wished to cross regularly from one bank to another. Probably the best known is recorded in Greek mythology and is that over the River Styx which encircled the Underworld. Here the ferryman, Charon, transported the souls of the dead across its waters.

Although the subject is vast, when I was asked to write this book I decided to concentrate, in the main, on ferries in the coastal areas including certain of those which involved crossing an "arm of the sea", spending more time on those which especially interested me and which could be easily reached by a non-car driver like myself. It is inevitable that I have been obliged to omit some which readers may think should have been included, and to the operators and users of these I offer my apologies.

A few of the books on the subject are listed in the Bibliography and these and many others will provide additional reading. Local reference libraries can usually provide other interesting material on the subject to those wishing to expand their knowledge beyond that which it is possible to include within these pages.

I have found that there is confusion about and misuse of terms connected with maritime affairs. To call any vessel a boat, other than a small undecked open craft propelled by oars, lugsail or outboard engine, separately or in any combination, is inaccurate. Similarly I understand a wherry to be either a shallow draught decked sailing vessel that was used to carry freight on the Norfolk Broads, or a seventeenth/eighteenth century open boat once used on the tidal waters of the River Thames to carry passengers.

Both are cases where the definition, strictly speaking, has been applied inaccurately. The great majority of people using ferries are land based and have little or no connection with maritime affairs and consequently call their conveyance a ferry-boat. In fact the word ferry alone describes any vessel used to transport passengers and goods from one place to another on a regular service. Words such as wherry are used to describe craft that are only similar to a wherry and not the true thing. I give these two examples to show the sort of difficulty I encountered and hope I may be excused by those who claim that any description is not strictly accurate. The descriptions given are those that are used locally as far as my informants are concerned. It is important at the outset to define the term "ferry".

The *Encyclopaedia Britannica* gives two definitions:—

1. A place where boats ply regularly across a river or arm of the sea for the conveyance of goods and persons;
2. The boats employed in this manner.

These definitions are adhered to in the 1948 Report on Ferries prepared by the Committee appointed by the Minister of Transport. Its brief was to "investigate ferry services linking trunk and classified roads in Great Britain; to make recommendations for the improvement of the equipment or operation of such services with a view to their greater efficiency and adequacy, and, with the same object, to report as to any amendment of the law governing the provision of such services that appears to be desirable."

There are certain legalities regarding ferries with which the owner must comply. To quote from the report to the Minister of Transport:-

> "A right of ferry is an exclusive right to convey persons or goods (or both) across a river or arm of the sea and to charge reasonable tolls for the service. Goods may sometimes include vehicles. So long as the right is exercised the proprietor has a corresponding obligation to provide and maintain an adequate service and to restrict the tolls to such as are reasonable. However, the right must be exercised in such a way as not to interfere with ordinary navigation."

Some of the older ferries existed to satisfy local requirements and carried a limited amount of traffic. When this increased owners sometimes found it difficult to finance additional ferry facilities.

The Ferries Act of 1919 was therefore passed to empower local authorities in England and Wales to "purchase, or accept transfer of a legally established ferry, and to operate and improve the service." Scotland passed a similar Act in 1938—The Harbour, Piers and Ferries Act.

When the Department of Trade (D.o.T.) Committee made their investigations, forty-four vehicular river ferries, varying in importance and efficiency, were known to be in operation. The proprietors of these included local authorities and railway, dock, harbour and canal authorities.

At the time of the Report a legally established river ferry in England or Wales could be extinguished only by Act of Parliament, while in Scotland this could be done by the proprietor notifying the County Council of his intention.

An article in the *Journal of Commerce*, dated April 1957, "Open Spaces and Footpaths Preservation Society," explains the procedure:—

> "Where the highway is a franchise ferry, the owner of the ferry has an important right and a still more important obligation to operate and maintain the ferry.
>
> The obligation may seem harsh in modern times, when ferries are so much less used than they were . . . the operation of a ferry cannot be

dismissed as a financial burden unless the owner has at least made application for a grant from the Minister of Transport . . .

The example set by Durham County Council in the present session of Parliament (April 1957) provides the appropriate answer. The County Council has promoted a Private Members Bill in order to extinguish the Barnston/Coxgrove Ferry, and incidentally the Bill provides for a footbridge to be built. Not all ferries can readily be replaced by bridges nor is it always necessary that there should be any kind of substitute . . . What the Society does consider to be essential is that, if any owner of a franchise ferry wishes to restrict, replace or discontinue the ferry services he should do so in a lawful and not in an arbitrary manner. He should . . . seek his ends by approved legislation."

Bernard Wood, in his excellent book—*Ferries and Ferrymen*—describes the ferryman's pivotal character to be "as essential to the life of the community as the parson or bobby."

Mention has already been made of the use of ferries for the carriage of animals. What of the people who use them?

The ferry over the Firth of Forth, since replaced by the Forth Road Bridge, was named the Queensferry after Queen Margaret, who frequently used it in the tenth century when she encouraged pilgrims to visit the shrine of Saint Andrew in Fife, crossing the river at the narrows of Inchgarvie. Later, her youngest son, David I, instituted a regular ferry service granting the rights to the monks at Dunfermline.

Charles I, before his accession, crossed the Gravesend/Tilbury Ferry, then known as Cross Ferry, when he went to Spain to woo the Spanish Infanta.

In his *Tour Through England and Wales,* written about 1724, Daniel Defoe describes his experience when landing on the Lancashire side of Woodside Ferry:—

"Here is a ferry over the Mersee, which, at full sea, is more than two miles over. We land on the flat shore on the other side, and are contented to ride through the water for some length, not on horseback, but on the shoulders of some honest Lancashire clown, who comes knee deep to the boat side, to truss you up, and then runs away with you as nimbly as you desire to ride, unless his trot were easier; for I was so shaken by him that I had the luck to be carry'd by more than I car'd for, and much worse than a hard trotting horse would have shaken me."

John Wesley, the famous Methodist preacher, crossed many ferries in the course of his preaching tours throughout England and Wales. In May 1753 he records that after preaching at Pocklington, in Yorkshire, he rode on to Whitgift Ferry.

"It rained a great part of the way and just as we got to the water a furious shower began, which continued above half an hour while we were striving to get John Haines' horse into the boat, but we were forced, after all, to leave him behind."

And again, when returning from Cornwall in 1768, he writes in his Journal: —

> "When we came to Crimble passage", today known as Cremyll, "we were at a full stop. The boatman told us the storm was too high, that it was not possible to pass; however, at length we persuaded them to venture out and we did not ship one sea till we got over."

Still another record in this traveller's diary refers to his experience at Tattershall, in Lincolnshire. The date was July 1781 when he "met with such a ferry as I never saw before. The boat was managed by an honest countryman who knew just nothing of the matter, and a young woman equally skilful. However, though the river was fifty yards broad we got over it in an hour and a half."

William Gilpin gives the following vivid description of approaching and crossing the Severn New Passage from Chessel Pil to Portskewett in 1770: — "A miserable walk we had through sludge and over shelving and slippery rocks. When we got to it we found eleven horses on board and above thirty people, and our chaise, which we had intended to convert into a cabin during the voyage, was slung into the shrouds. The boat, after some struggling with the shelves, at length gained the channel after beating about near two hours against the wind. Our voyage concluded, as it had begun, with an uncomfortable walk through the sludge to high water mark."

In the nineteenth century the ferry between East and West Cowes was known as "the Queen's Ferry." Visitors and local people waited to see Queen Victoria's landau, with scarlet favours and outriders, halt at the crossing when she made her journey to and from Osborne on the Isle of Wight.

During the Second World War Queen Mary often crossed the Aust/Beachley Ferry when staying at Badminton, while in still more recent times, Queen Elizabeth, the Queen Mother, used this ferry.

Although there were many complaints about the delays, discomforts and dangers, ferrymen have worked their craft in all weathers, at all times of day and night, however inadequate or primitive their vessels may have been.

In spite of accidents and delays, ferries were, and still are a necessity. With modern aids to navigation serious accidents are so few that ferries are one of the pleasantest means of travel and also the safest.

The East/West Cowes chain ferry at East Cowes in 1890.

CHAPTER ONE

Crossing the Waters

Southern and Western England, Wales and North West England

ALTHOUGH ferries operated before Roman times the Doomsday Book (1085) was probably the first record of the existence of such ferries, many of which may have been of more ancient origin.

In the Department of Trade Report already referred to, the Investigation Committee stated that the origin of the right of ferry was, in some cases, so obscure that the date of creation was unknown, but such information as was available usually pointed to creation by Royal Grant or by Act of Parliament.

A ferry may seem a simple arrangement whereby somebody with a boat plies for hire from a given point on one side of a river or estuary to the opposite side. But it is very much more than that. A franchise is a legal right to ply for hire; protected by the law from competition from others and coupled with a duty, which may be enforced in the Courts, to carry all wayfarers across the river. By franchise is meant an exclusive privilege in the hands of a subject which arises generally from a Royal Grant or from prescription which pre-supposes a grant. There are various kinds of franchise but that of the ferry is perhaps the most fascinating, largely because it is a curious link with our historic past.

Now let us consider the origin, ownership and history of different types of ferry which have interested me around the country, starting close to my home in the south and travelling around the coast, starting in a westerly direction.

In a little book entitled—*All About Bury*—Lilian Brown, a former resident, reminds us that the original date of the **Bury Ferry,** Sussex, over the Arun, is uncertain but an account of 1392 shows 5s. 0d. rent for the farm of the ferry (passegium) with the boat. One bushel, probably a bushel of corn, was charged for taking the lords' servants across the water as often as necessary. This was when Bury was in the hands of the sovereign. The ferry boat appears to have been provided and kept in repair by Arundel Estate and replaced when necessary with a new one built in their own yards.

Bury Church was built close to the ferry and in 1533 John Luttard left 2d. to "St. Christofer's Light" in Bury Church, which suggests that the church paid reverence to Saint Christopher whose statue occupied a niche on the north side of the chancel.

Luttards lived in the parish for about three hundred years and the bequest could possibly have been made as a token of gratitude for safe passage over the river. As Saint Christopher was known as the patron saint of travellers passengers doubtless asked for the Saint's protection before crossing by the ferry.

A registry entry concerning William Webb, Waterman, married in 1851, suggests he may have worked the ferry at that time, the term "waterman" or "ferryman" often being synonymous. Appointments were made by Arundel and a house went with the office.

Mrs Shepherd, one of a long-standing family in Bury, was still remembered by older parishioners in 1948 as a "true Sussex character who would work the ferry as good as any man." One of her many daughters, Mrs Marshall, afterwards carried on the ferry with the assistance of her family. "Bob" Dudden, who succeeded her, was a popular ex-naval man. The ferry has long since ceased to function.

It is not surprising to find that a number of ferries crossed Southampton Water. Many were of ancient origin, possibly dating back to Roman times.

At **Itchen**, Hampshire, for example, ferry rights have been granted from time immemorial.

Said to be owned by the Bishops of Winchester, then the lords of the manor of Bittern, the ferry was leased out to private people with local sailors employed as ferrymen. Much later, in 1834, the Itchen Bridge Company was formed, purchasing the rights to the profits of the ferry for £7,000.

In 1948 the Department of Trade Committee reported that the ferry was the connecting link between the central area of Southampton and Woolston, the nearest alternative crossing being Northam Bridge, two miles away up the river. Their conclusion was that in view of the traffic importance of this route there should be a permanent crossing. Since then, of course, the Itchen Bridge has been built. It was opened on 13th July, 1977. It cost twelve million pounds, but in the first week 55,635 vehicles crossed the bridge and £6,000 in toll money was taken. But it has to be added that this vastly increased the traffic on the approach roads.

It is thought that substantial vessels equipped for rowing and sailing, known locally as wherries, were used in the early days on Itchen Ferry, but 1836 saw the steam ferry brought into commission. Mudie in his *History of Hampshire* described the ferry as "one of the neatest and most enormous boat passages in Europe across which carriages, coaches, teams and all manner of wheeled vehicles are conducted without disturbing one buckle of their harness, or an article of their load. Riders have no occasion to dismount and foot passengers may, if they choose, find shelter in the saloons, while all may regale themselves at the usual cost, with fruits, pastry and beverages.

The boat is a broad punt with the cabins and machinery in the centre, a carriage way at each side and a platform at each end . . . the action is produced by steam."

The Department of Trade Report described the craft in service in 1948 as follows:- "The equipment is of the pontoon and cable type, mechanically operated. There are three units of which two are in operation and the other is in reserve. The capacity of each craft is 10 cars. The service is operated day and night."

The **Hythe Ferry**, Hampshire, across the River Test at Southampton, which connects the Watergate Quay with the ancient Hard at Hythe, is still in service. It has operated since medieval times when the ferry rights belonged to Southampton Corporation, enabling travellers to continue their journey in a south-westerly direction to such places as Beaulieu, Lymington and Fawley. However, the Corporation appears to have lost these privileges many years ago.

Litigation during 1822/3 established the fact that Hythe was within the limits of the port of Southampton and this gave the Southampton Harbour Board some jurisdiction over development there, but in 1842 a Harbour Board Minute states that the boatmen need not be licensed by them in order to carry passengers between Hythe and Southampton.

An Act of Parliament which received the Royal Assent on 19th July 1844 empowered the Hythe Hard Company to take the existing public Hard, and to build a landing place or Hard within ten years of the passing of the Act. All watermen had to be licensed and the Company were given the right to collect tolls of 1d. per passenger, plus 1d. per ton for ships, from all using the Hard or landing within half a mile either side of the Hard.

When the Act was passed the watermen with their vessels were the mainstay of the service. The ownership and operation of the ferry changed hands several times in the course of the next forty years as companies failed financially. The present company came into being on 15th December 1874, its first cumbersome title — Hythe Pier and Hythe and Southampton Ferry Company Limited — being changed in 1923 to Hythe Pier Company Limited, which holds today.

The power to purchase the rights of the previous owner was not exercised until 1879. Hythe Pier Company now only own the pier, the ferry service being provided by the General Estates Company Limited, who operate the pier railway under lease from the Pier Company. The two companies are closely linked.

An interesting advertisement with regard to the tolls charged on the Hythe Ferry appeared in the Southampton Directory of 1836 headed —

Hoverlloyd's Hovercraft *Swift* which operated from Southampton to Cowes in the Isle of Wight.

British Hovercraft Corporati

"Steam Communication between Southampton, Hythe, Beaulieu, Lymington, the New Forest, etc."

It reads: —

"The public are respectfully informed that the beautiful new and complete Iron Steam Boat *Forester* (8 h. p.) (Built expressly for the Station), will, on and after Monday, July 25th 1836, leave Hythe for Southampton every morning at seven o'clock and every hour after till eight in the evening; and the Royal Pier, Southampton for Hythe at half past seven and every hour after, till half past eight in the evening.

The *Forester* is well fitted with fore and aft cabins, and every accommodation required for the passage, and the Proprietors earnestly solicit that patronage and support which they hope will be given to those who commence undertakings for the better accommodation of the public.

Fares — after cabin 6d.
fore cabin 3d.

Including the charge for landing and embarking at the Royal Pier."

The fares charged on the ferry in 1887 where 10d. return and 6d. single first class, second class fares were 7d. and 4d. respectively.

By 1970, however, return tickets ceased to be issued and the fares rose to 10p (2/-) (boat) and 1½p (3½d. approx.) (train), while in January 1977 the Company issued a new time-table with the statement that higher expenses on fuel, oil, harbour dues and wages would necessitate increased fares but the train would be free for passengers using the ferry when seats were available.

Starting with the *Forester* in 1836, twelve more steam boats have been in operation, including the present fleet of ferries owned and operated by the General Estates Company. These include three *Hotspurs, II, III* and *IV*, all built by the Rowhedge Ironworks Ltd., Essex, who built many boats for the Company. They each had diesel engines and carried from 300 to 350 passengers.

The *Carrick Lass*, wooden built, and purchased by the Company in 1937 to assist with the service, was taken over by the Admiralty in 1940 and sent to West Africa as deck cargo, but was lost en route when the ship was sunk.

For many years the ferries were painted with a black hull, having a black funnel with a white band. In June 1963 *Hotspur IV* was given a blue-coloured hull and the funnel was repainted in cream with a white band and these colours were later adopted for the other two ferries with slightly different shades of the same colours.

Hotspur III and *IV* were re-engined in 1969 and 1968 respectively, enabling the engines to be controlled from the bridge. The ferry is now operated by two crews comprising a skipper, mate and engineer each, one crew working from 7 a.m. until midday, when the other crew takes over. An additional boat comes into service from 4.45 p.m. for the benefit of commuters.

Further westward along the south coast two other ancient ferries cross the River Stour. It is thought that the ferry across the Stour must have been in use before the College of Augustinian Canons was founded, about the eleventh or twelfth centuries.

The **Wick Ferry**, Dorset, leaves the landing stage at the end of Wick Lane on the Christchurch side and runs to the landing stage on the Wick side. It was the property of the Lord of the Manor of Christchurch and known as Knaptons and Holloways, since when it has had a succession of owners. It probably existed for centuries as the only direct communication between Wick village and the town of Christchurch. There was no direct road or bridge until a private company built one at Tuckton in 1882. Eli Miller and his family kept the ferry in operation from 1800 until 1903.

This ferry was discontinued on several occasions because it was running at a loss. Mr Stride, the current ferryman and his two brothers, purchased the boat rights in 1970. The ferry, a motor boat, is licensed to carry twelve passengers, but it does not run in the winter months. Originally started for the benefit of school children, it now serves the adjacent holiday camp and other summer visitors.

The other ferry across the Stour was the **Redhill Ferry**, originally known as Riddles Ferry, which occupied the site of a ford about half a mile down stream from West Parley. It is believed the Roman legions used this ford on their way to attack the British at Badbury Rings, near Wimborne. The ford was once known as Riddlesford (Redhill Ford). This place name appears on several maps dating from 1791.

Passengers were pulled across the river by a rope at Redhill; earlier they had been poled across in a punt. A Bournemouth librarian told me that, at one time, the tea gardens from which the ferry operated belonged to her grandparents, Mr and Mrs Charles Marshall. Mrs Marshall often used to operate the ferry and serve teas in the gardens. The ferry was the only link between West Parley and Bournemouth. Before the road bridge was built traffic not using the ferry had to go by the ancient bridge at Longham, Dorset.

For several centuries **Poole Ferry** was the only means of communication across the channel dividing Hamworthy from Poole. The ferry is still much in demand especially with visitors wishing to cross to Shell Bay. A lease, dated May 1541, is the earliest document relating to the ferry, which saves the motorist 25 miles on a return journey from Bournemouth to Swanage, but the ferry did not become financially sound until after the Second World War. Local fishermen brought people across before the ferry was established.

Tom Davies, a retired ferryman and shipbuilder living in Poole, told me his father was running a rowing boat across the Poole Ferry when he was fifteen years of age. Tom himself started when he was about fourteen. When he took over the boat he installed a Seagull outboard motor.

It was the ferryman's responsibility to insure the boats against damage and to maintain them in good repair. Apart from any retainer which might be given, he had to rely entirely on what was given by the passengers.

During the Second World War troops were the only users of this ferry and it was not re-opened until 12th July 1946. On that day Hants and Dorset Company buses went into service across the ferry and a group of cyclists, pedestrians and motorists made immediate use of it. Tom's brother ran the Poole to Hamworthy Ferry before the 1914 war and afterwards. He used a rowing boat and had to row against the tide all day long, but only one accident was recorded and that during a gale. At night pilots rowed people across, bartering a charge for the return journey on their one boat.

Two of the boats were used in the evacuation of Dunkirk. Tom took the *Felicity* to Dover and towed her back to Poole after she had completed her usefulness at Dunkirk. The second boat, *The Island Queen,* was lost and had to be replaced at a cost five or ten times as much as previously paid. It is not known how she was lost but she never returned.

Today the Bournemouth-Swanage Motor Road and Ferry Company are the operators of the ferry service, as they have been for more than fifty years.

Mr Aman, whose family ran the ferry from 1926, had the first steam driven ferry built at a cost of £12,000. Although there were problems of maintaining steam during the crossing in bad weather the steam ferry remained in service until 1958 when the current ferry came into service. This was a 350-ton diesel-powered cabin ferry (floating bridge), with space for 28 vehicles and 200 passengers. Besides being faster, cleaner and more economic to run this made it possible to handle a 60 per cent increase in vehicular traffic, with a potential rise in traffic receipts of £13,000 for the operational year. The chains were of high tensile steel. The ferry operates continuously throughout the day from 7 a.m. until 11 p.m., summer and winter, the only exceptions being Christmas Day, New Year's Day and Sundays in the winter.

The ferry route cuts across a busy area but there has never been a serious accident although there have been some near misses, mainly with inexperienced week-end sailing people.

In 1975 1,235,000 passengers, nearly 500,000 cars and 15,000 buses and coaches were conveyed on the ferry, which makes it economically sound, although it never was financially successful until after the Second World War.

In *Memorials of Exmouth* (1872) reference is made to the **Exmouth Ferry** "across the river to Starcross, where you can pick up the South Devon Railway and go where it pleases." In fact, by using the ferry, foot passengers wishing to go west from Exmouth are saved the long slow journey via Exeter and the delay occasioned by changing trains.

W. G. Hoskins states, in his book *Devon—A new Survey of England,* that "from 1122 Sherborne Abbey, in Dorset, had possessed the Manor of Littleham on the eastern side of the Exe mouth and they developed a regular ferry across the estuary from the fishing hamlet of Exmouth to a landing place now called Star Cross in the Manor of Kenton."

The old Sandbanks—Shell Bay ferry. *T. S. Davis's Collection*

For several centuries continual disputes concerning ownership of the ferry took place between the Abbot and Convent of Sherborne and the Manor and Bailiffs of Exeter. Eventually it was agreed that Exeter citizens had a right to the passage and ferry and that the "lastage, stallage, and petty customs (town duties) landed and discharged within the limits of the Port of Exeter were the property of the said citizens as being a parcel of the said city, held of the Duchy of Cornwall, by fee-farm rent of £20 a year, payable at the said Duchy Court."

A small vessel still plies several times a day during the summer season between Starcross and Exmouth. It covers the route that has been followed since the twelfth century.

In October 1887 the Corporation of Exeter leased the ferry to John Picard, at an annual rent of 44s. He was under obligation to keep in good repair the houses and boats belonging to the ferry.

A local guide book of 1899 referred to a pontoon for the conveyance of horses and carriages and other vehicles across the river from Exmouth to Starcross, but no information has been found elsewhere about this. The first boat specially built to carry passengers across the estuary to Starcross was the *Melita*. This was in 1894. At that time between 90,000 and 100,000 passengers were carried in one season.

A later boat, the *Starcross*, was on war duty in 1939.

Prior to 1965 consideration was given to establishing a car ferry, but tidal conditions and cost were factors against any such action.

There was a ferry at **Topsham**, which is bounded on the west by the river Exe and on the east by the Clyst, the two rivers meeting just below the town. It was owned and operated by the landlord of the *Passage House*, or *Ferry Inn.*

At Dartmouth in Devon there have been three ferries across the River Dart, the Lower Ferry probably being of the oldest foundation. An Act passed in 1830 allowed the Higher Ferry to establish a floating bridge across Dartmouth harbour.

The **Dartmouth to Kingswear Ferry,** between that known locally as "the railway station without rails" at Dartmouth and the Kingswear railway pier, dated only from 1864 when Dartmouth and Torbay Railway Company's short line was opened.

The first ferry for the Dartmouth Kingswear passage over the River Dart was built in 1831 by Sir John Seale and his son, Henry Paul Seale. A horse, walking around in a rotunda amidships, turned machinery which winched the ferry across on chains. This was changed to steam propulsion by Philip & Son of Dartmouth in 1867 and was operated by driving on two chains anchored to each bank. In 1920 this was replaced by a larger ferry with a deck 55 feet long by 32 feet wide. It carried eight to ten cars in two lanes and was driven by a steam engine taken from the 1867 version. Propulsion was by paddles. This was replaced in 1960 by the present diesel electric ferry, deck measurements being 84 feet by 32 feet with capacity for eighteen cars. The chains were replaced by cables.

The approximate annual traffic on this ferry is: 23,000 pedestrians, 20,000 motor cycles, combinations and cycles, 325,000 cars and vans, 10,000 lorries and coaches and 34,000 coach passengers, making a total of 412,000 passengers and vehicles.

After taking a party of people to visit the National Trust's Devon property near **Salcombe**, Mr Dennis Thomas wrote in the Trust's magazine "Whenever a crossing of water was involved, even if it was a short ferry trip, this always added colour to an outing. A walk over Trust clifflands from Bolt Tail to Bolt Head, followed by a sea estuary trip up the Sal from Smugglers Cove into Salcombe, was memorable for me by the ferry owner collecting his cash for the party at sea, which he insisted on doing before allowing anyone to land. I, with the money, was in the other boat from the owner, and remember my concern whilst standing amidships on a boat which was rising and falling considerably in a somewhat choppy sea, whilst the owner tried to count the heads of our party. This was a task he set himself which was quite impossible to fulfill, as there were other passengers in one ferry who were not of our party. After giving up, he took my word for our number. I then had to try to pass a £5 note, fluttering in the breeze in my hand, overboard to him. I felt that I got even with this by insisting upon his handing me back the correct change, which he finally did."

An unusual ferry is that which operates between **Bigbury and Burgh Island**, Devon. Here, when the tide recedes, there is a wide path of firm sand between the two points, so that those wishing to cross to the island can walk there. The ferry, variously described as a Sea Tractor or a Sea Horse, operates only when the tide is in. It serves holiday makers, proprietors, and guests staying at the hotel on the island or wishing to take refreshment at the *Pilchard Inn*.

Many well-known people have travelled on the Sea Tractor and stayed at the hotel, one being Agatha Christie, who wrote two novels while there, *Evil Under the Sun* and *Ten Little Nigger Boys*.

The owners of the twenty-four acres of island, the hotel, the inn and the Sea Tractor, are Tom and Sue Waugh, who purchased it from the Bigbury Bay Holiday Company and took possession in June 1968. The hotel is open from Easter until the end of September. During the winter the "ferry" is taken out of the water.

The present Sea Tractor was purchased after Tom and Sue bought the Island. The one previously in use, from 1948, was sent to the Museum for Public Transport Vehicles at Wimple.

When I met Tom and his manager at the *Pilchard Inn* they told me that approximately six hundred people travel on the Sea Tractor a day during the

The Sea Tractor Ferry linking Bigbury-on-Sea with Burgh Island.
From colour print by Photo Precision Limited, St Ives, Cambs.

summer. A strange-looking contraption, it stands on four very large wheels so that the box-like passenger accommodation above, covered by an awning and approached by a flight of steps, is well clear of the water. It runs on diesel fuel with transmission through hydraulics. There is a half-hourly service during the summer months, with a charge of 10p for adults and half price for children. Hotel guests do not pay for the service.

Most of the Cornish ferries are very ancient and have an interesting history. They were created because this was the only means of overcoming the obstacles caused by the many rivers with estuaries along Cornwall's southern coast.

Cremyll Ferry and Saltash, linking Devon and Cornwall across the Tamar, were among the oldest and most important, with records going back to the eleventh and twelfth centuries. Douglas C. Vosper, in *The Ancient Ferry at Saltash*, writes that the ferry and the right of crossing and landing goes back into antiquity. Tradition has it that the women of Saltash rowed the Black Prince across the passage to join his troops and then secured for the inhabitants the right of the crossing and of landing for half a mile up and down the stream.

Cremyll linked Stonehouse and Plymouth and was the main link from Devon to the southernmost of the three Cornish roads. The first owners appearing in the records were the Valletort family. Later this ferry came into the hands of the Mount Edgcumbe family.

By the end of the seventeenth century traffic had greatly increased on Cremyll Ferry which was carrying the mail for most of Cornwall, but it was a hazardous passage, with three tides meeting.

Crossings were not only hazardous, they were uncomfortable, as that intrepid woman traveller, Celia Fiennes found when, in 1694, she crossed on the Cremyll Ferry.

> "Had I known the danger before I should not have been very willing to have gone it, not but this is the constant way all people go, and saved several miles riding. I was at least an hour going over; it was about a mile, but indeed in some places, notwithstanding there were five men rowed and I set my own man to row also, I do believe we made not a step of way for almost a quarter of an hour, but blessed be God, I came safely over but those ferry boats are so wet and then the sea and wind are always cold to be upon, that I never fail to catch cold in a ferry boat."*

The new passage of 1730 from Cremyll to Devil's Point, and the additional route to Mutton Cove, introduced in 1724 were, like the old passage, not without their dangers. Steamboats were safer than open boats with sails and oars, but they could not always cope with the hazards of wind and weather. One resident wrote to a newspaper:

> "Dense fog over the estuary, characteristic of an autumn morning following a hot day, known locally as a 'river gale' (an indication of a stormy, wet day to follow, and coinciding with a strong ebb tide . . .) often put the ferry off course and caused difficulty in locating the landing place. Occasionally these elements resulted in the ferry being stranded at Admiral's Hard where she had to remain until the turn of the tide in the afternoon to float her off. The ferry had to be supported by blocks to prevent her breaking her back . . . During very high tides and rough weather, especially in spring and autumn, landing at Cremyll was impossible, and was made in the Cremyll Yard."

Cremyll did not have a steamboat until 1889. The *Carrier* was the largest of the three in use in the early years of this century. Her engines were powerful and gave her a speed of ten knots and she carried two masts, had a crew of three and could carry 150 passengers.

* *Through England on a Side Saddle in the time of William and Mary, 1695-97.* Celia Fiennes.

The *Armadillo* was smaller than the *Carrier* but similar in build. She had an upright funnel and one mast. She also had a crew of three and could carry 108 passengers.

The *Shuttlecock* was older and smaller than the other two; it has been suggested that she was built in the 1870's, but the date seems a little uncertain. Her build was similar to that of the *Carrier* and the *Armadillo*, although she was distinguished by a black funnel. She broke from her moorings in a storm in 1910 and was wrecked on the shore at Mount Wise.

The *Shuttlecock* and *Armadillo* were open at the bow and not decked in; there were occasions when anxiety was caused by the amount of water shipped during stormy crossings. On one occasion the *Shuttlecock* only just reached Cremyll in time to prevent her sinking.

Mr E. Porter, of Millbrook, remembered an incident before the First World War when, during a very severe gale, as the only passanger crossing from Stonehouse to Cremyll on a late evening trip, the Captain handed him a life belt and said: "You had better put this on—I doubt if we will reach the other side." They did, but only after a severe drenching.

The *Carrier* and the *Armadillo* were broken up in 1927 and two new wooden boats, propelled by steam and of similar design, though slightly longer, were built in the same year. These new boats were named *Armadillo* and *Shuttlecock*.

For many years the conveyance of horses and carts had been in another boat towed behind the ferry and this continued long after the introduction of steam. A letter dated 10th March 1903 contains a specification and quotation for a new horseboat for the Earl of Mount Edgcumbe. The measurements were 36 feet × 10 feet 2 inches × 3 feet 9 inches. The cost was to be £14.18s. if the bottom of the boat was tarred, felted and coppered; £12. 15s. if the bottom was caulked and treated with pitch and tar. It came in stern first, having a ramp for unloading and could carry two four-wheeled carts and their horses, or horses alone.

It was not unknown for the tow rope to the horseboat to break during stormy weather and serious delays were sometimes experienced in picking up the almost unmanageable horse transporter. The increased use of motor haulage during the 20s and 30s, however, and the greater facilities offered by the Torpoint Ferry for a quicker trip to Plymouth, led to a gradual decline in the use of the boat. An engineer on the ferry boats at that time thinks that shortly after January 1940 the horse transporter either broke away or was lost, for on his return from naval service in 1945 there was no trace of it.

The Millbrook Steamboat Company managed the Cremyll Ferry from 1943 and bought the boats from the Mount Edgcumbe Estate in June 1945, at which time the ferries were converted from steam to diesel. The *Armadillo* (II) was fitted with a Kelvin diesel engine and renamed *Northern Belle*. The

Shuttlecock (II) had a complete conversion at the Cremyll Yard and was fitted with a top deck for passengers and a Glennifer diesel engine. Renamed the *Southern Belle* she made her maiden voyage in July 1946 and was then used primarily for river excursions from Plymouth. In 1957 the Millbrook Steamboat Company purchased the *May Queen* from the Plymouth and Creston Steamboat Company and renamed it the *Eastern Belle*. She was used alternately with the *Northern Belle* on the Cremyll Ferry and had a Thornycroft engine.

There was no serious competition with rival ferries, the object being to keep a public service open and for the ferry to show a profit, but no more than this.

Early in Victoria's reign there were at least seventeen crossings of the Tamar from Halton in Calstock to Penlee Point, to say nothing of those in Sutton Pool and to the east of Plymouth.

In 1948 the Department of Trade Report stated that the Saltash ferry was still operating and the bulk of the traffic consisted of private cars and commercial vehicles. The volume of traffic was increased by fifty per cent during the summer months but even in winter occasionally there was a congestion of traffic on the approach roads, the greater part being through traffic likely to increase rather than diminish in volume. The Committee therefore recommended that the ferry service should again operate at the pre-war intervals of twenty minutes rather than the half-hourly service introduced in the post-Second World War years.

The Report also added that only the construction of a road bridge, which the Council was considering, would effectively meet the potential traffic demands. This has since been done, with the consequent closing of the ferry. Now there is only the Torpoint/Devonpoint Ferry, but that is very active and important, saving a detour for traffic of sixteen miles by road.

The **Torpoint Ferry**, across the Tamar to Devonport, was not opened as a boat ferry until 1791 following the Act of 1790, although some form of unofficial ferry may have been in use prior to that time, as with the growth of Plymouth Dock there was need for a regular ferry service at this point for the benefit of dockyard workers, naval personnel, traders and others living in the developing town of Torpoint.

The new Act which was passed concerning the operation of this ferry stated that the Earl of Mount Edgcumbe and Reginald Pole Carew, who held the ferry rights, were ready and willing, at their own charges, to build and provide, maintain and keep a competent number of substantial boats for use on the ferry, with a sufficient number of capable and experienced ferrymen. They were also willing to erect necessary and proper wharves and landing places and buildings for the purpose, and, with the authorisation of Parliament, demand and receive rates for passage and conveyance.

In 1793 Walter Cross took the *Ferry House Inn* at Torpoint announcing "a sufficient number of convenient boats and able men kept in readiness for to carry over coaches and other carriages." Competition from other ferry operators was keen and unscrupulous. Within weeks it was being said, and later reported in the newspapers, that Cross's ferry boat had overturned and three passengers drowned during a violent gale. Cross promptly denied the rumour and declared it had been circulated by one of his rivals.

In 1802, at the *London Inn*, Torpoint, Cross announced that in September he was "keeping two horse-boats, each manned by three men and two foot boats constantly plying during the usual hours of the day."

These ferries were of the simplest construction — a wooden platform fixed catamaran-like to hulls. A drawing of c. 1660 shows such a ferry crossing the river Fowey from Bodinnick. Apart from this particular service and until 1827 the Torpoint Ferry was worked by rowing and sailing boats for horse traffic and pedestrians. There were two horse boats and two foot boats. The ferry boat plied between the hours of 6 a.m. and 9 p.m. in summer and 7 a.m. and 8 p.m. in winter. Great inconvenience was frequently caused by contrary winds and tides which prolonged the crossing time.

The first Torpoint steam ferry was launched at Hockens Yard at Stonehouse with great ceremony on 29th September 1829 after a private Company had obtained the lease of the ferry. Named the *Jemima*, she was 70 feet long, 25 feet beam, powered by two 12 h.p. engines, and constructed to enable carriages and waggons to drive on and off without unharnessing the horses. The *Jemima* commenced service in February 1831 but proved to have insufficient power to overcome the strong tidal current thereby causing frustrating delays to the ferry time table. She was soon withdrawn from service and a return was made to the old two boat system. The proprietors, still searching for the ideal mechanical ferry, approached a Mr James Rendell who had successfully designed ferries at Dartmouth and Dundee. Mr Rendell considered the difficulties and built the chain ferry steam bridge which was opened to the public in 1834.

Landing places on either side of the river extended two feet beyond the high water mark to two feet beyond the low water mark at a gradient of 1 in 14. As the ferry approached the end ramp was lowered until it touched the landing place. The depth of water under the ferry and the projection of the ramps were so regulated that the carriages and horses were embarked or disembarked dry, while the ferry was, at the same time, afloat and in no danger of grounding. The crew of the ferry consisted of two men, one to tend the engines, the other to raise and lower the ramps and keep a look-out for other traffic on the river. The tolls were collected at toll houses on either shore. Fully loaded the ferry only drew about 2 feet 6 inches of water and the hull, practically flat for about 30 feet, sloped gently upwards towards each end. The ferry crossed the river four times in an hour and took eight minutes at high tide (2,550 feet) and 7 minutes at low tide (2,110 feet) to cross.

For two years there was only one ferry, but in 1836 another was acquired with its own set of chains so that both could operate independently. This was found to be more economical than the constant use of one ferry, as repairs could be carried out more effectively.

In July 1922, when the Cornwall County Council acquired the ferry undertaking, two floating bridges and two steam launches were in operation but these were practically worn out.

Philip & Son, of Dartmouth, built two new ferry bridges from designs by Mr T. P. Endean, then Ferry Manager at Torpoint. The first came into service in 1925, replacing a bridge which had been in operation for fifty-four years. The second, a floating bridge of similar size, was purchased in 1926 replacing one which had been in use for forty-eight years.

Although these new bridges were substantially the same in principle to those used in 1835, their construction was greatly improved. They provided

The Bodinnick Ferry in Cornwall. *From colour print by John Hinde Limited, Co Dublin.*

accommodation for 800 people and about 26 cars of average size and cost £14,650 and £20,000 respectively.

In March 1956 the County Council considered alternative designs, submitted by various shipbuilders, for new ferry bridges providing up to approximately 50 per cent increases in carrying capacity and decided to purchase two new bridges of increased carrying capacity with diesel-electric motive power.

In 1959 the Ferry Committee accepted the tender of John I. Thornycroft, Southampton, for the construction and delivery of two new bridges at a total cost of approximately £315,000. These were of robust construction and designed to carry vehicles of all the usual types as well as providing spacious accommodation for a large number of passengers. Special attention was given to the design of hinged prows to enable long wheel-base vehicles, such a motor coaches, to embark and disembark, fully laden, without the use of wheel-boards.

Mr Heneghan, the Chief Engineer at Torpoint, told me that today the ferry is free to passengers. It runs every seven minutes and yet there were long queues waiting in most of the seven lanes at Torpoint when I crossed before 10 a.m. in October 1977. Tide and fog do not affect the ferry and although the Harbour Master can shut the Harbour in certain fog conditions the ferry can still move.

In August 1958 the ferry was out of action for seven hours. It happened just before the evening rush hour and by 9 o'clock, 120 vehicles were reported waiting, a coach having to wait for three hours before crossing, although the north ferry was running a shuttle service during the breakdown period. This was the first time in two years one of these 20-ton chains had broken. To repair it and get the ferry going again, two workmen stood neck-deep in the Tamar; this typifies the attitude of the workers who keep the ferry going.

However, I am informed by Mr Mather that the ferry has not suffered broken chains since changing from iron to steel in 1958. Despite the great amount of traffic which uses the ferries, breakdowns are comparatively rare.

A day time service ferry runs throughout the year, while the night service ferry runs from 10.30 p.m. to 5 a.m., a half-hourly service during the early part of the night with an hourly service later. To cope with increased traffic a third ferry comes into daytime service during the summer and operates until November.

Motor cycles and priority use Lane 7 on the Torpoint side. When ambulances come into the emergency lane (Lane 7A) the man in the tower puts the lights to green to pass them through quickly. According to the nature of the emergency the ferry will either continue to load cars up to the full load, or, if it is a matter of life and death, will leave at once, even if the ambulance is the only vehicle on the ferry. At night, when an ambulance comes down to the embarkation point with its blue light glowing, the crew bring the ferry in from where it has been moored slightly away from the beach, and take the ambulance across immediately.

Torpoint has had its changes of ownership, its problems and mishaps; also its improvements and expansions, but it is probably one of the busiest and most successful of these river ferries in operation today.

The thirteenth century **Polruan Ferry** in Cornwall is run by Jack Toms, the local boat builder. The slipway on the Bodinnick side belongs to Toms; that on the other side belongs to the County Council.

A crew of three man the two vessels, one of which carries eight cars while the smaller carries six. When the weather is very rough the ferry does not run. Passengers are mainly business men, teachers and school children. Ships and dredgers have the right of way and sound their sirens when approaching the ferry passage. A chain ferry cannot be used on account of these ships passing up and down the river.

The passenger ferry is a small motor boat which runs winter and summer. In summer it runs up to 11 o'clock at night and in winter up to 10 o'clock. If a doctor is called out after the ferry has closed for the night he has to cross the river by the bridge at Lostwithiel, a 16 mile journey. In the old days sheep and cattle were transported on this ferry.

In 1732 ownership of the **Par to Bodinnick** passage and ferry boat was highly disputed between the Lords of Tywardneath and Mr Scobell of Roselyon. Now, however, the ferry has disappeared. It is filled over and covered with streets of houses: yet it was operating about two hundred years ago.

The **Bodinnick to Fowey Ferry** was mentioned in records in 1344 as belonging to the Manor of Bodinnick. The nearest alternative crossing is by the bridge at Lostwithiel, which is five miles by water.

The ferries are of the simplest construction—a wooden platform or float fixed catamaran-like to hulls and propelled by a motor boat alongside, plying between slipways. The first vehicle on is the first to land. The service is not operated at night.

The 1948 Committee recommended that the existing ferry should be replaced by new equipment and the Fowey terminal should be resited to provide more accommodation for waiting vehicles. A slight change had been made when I was there in October 1977 but the ferry was still of the same type though it is in keeping with the delightful old world atmosphere about the whole place, with its fascinating *Old Ferry Inn* on the Bodinnick side overlooking the river. Small wonder that Daphne du Maurier and also Arthur Quiller Couch found this an excellent setting for their novels. In his book, *Shining Ferry*, Quiller Couch has a fictitious character typical of one ferryman the author knew when he was living there.

The *Severn Princess* operating on the Aust to Beachley Ferry. In the background the Severn Bridge can be seen under construction. The Bridge replaced the Ferry. *P. Palmer*

The **King Harry Ferry** over the Truro River is one of the best known of the Cornish ferries. The origin of the name is not clear for there are many legends concerning it. Some believe King Henry VIII visited it and gave the name to it, but the real origin of the name is said to be in the dedication of the little chapel that stood in the Philleigh end of the passage. In 1528 this chapel was described as of St Mary and King Henry. "Clearly Henry VI is intended," says Charles Henderson, in his *Essays in Cornish History*, "so the ferry probably owes its name to the gentle Lancastrian rather than the blustering Tudor."

The ferry had a number of different tenants among the Lords of the Manor who, with their servants, had free passage on it, as did the vicar and his family, according to the old tithe customs of Feock.

This ferry has developed from a raft-like craft to a pontoon and chain type ferry, or floating bridge, now owned by the King Harry Steam Ferry Company. A 440-ton diesel ferry, it was built in Penryn in 1973. It is 188 feet long and caters for holiday and tourist traffic and local people travelling from home to Falmouth, Redruth and Truro on business or pleasure. Officially it accommodates 28 cars, but 50 or 60 could be put on, I am told. It carries ten life buoys and thirteen floatable boats. There is a crew of three and the skipper, who maintains the ferry. There is an eight foot tide here. The nearest alternative crossing is seven miles away by water.

The **Helford River** had its ancient ferry with its franchise giving it legal right to ply for hire and protected by law from competition from others. Originally it belonged to the Bishops of Exeter who had the manors of Minster and Penryn. Intending passengers hoisted a flag to attract the ferryman on the *Ferryboat Inn* side. Animals as well as passengers were conveyed across on the ferry and even a horse bus, which ran from Manacean to Falmouth, was transported on the ferry.

Another ferry of great antiquity is Jack the Ferrys, the name by which the passage across the **Hayle River** is known. This river effectively divided West Cornwall from the rest of the county except for the ferry. No one seems to know who this "Jack" was but the name has been used over the many years of the ferry's existence. Some think it is one of the oldest ferries in Cornwall, having been in operation before Hayle had become a township. It conveyed passengers across to the western side of the river thus giving them a short cut to Lelant and St Ives, though St Ives grew in importance as Lelant ceased to be an active seaport with the silting up of the river there.

In his book, *Beloved St Ives*, Cyril Noall writes of "the old ferryman who paddled his old flat-bottomed praam across the Hayle River from Lelant Towans to the beach on the Phillack side, 50, 60 and I expect 70 years ago . . . "

Another tourist says "If the tide had turned to got out, and a strong current was pouring out from Lelant mud, the ferryman and his praam would be swept down the stream as if 'twere but a straw. Notwithstanding this, not even the most ardent lovers from St Ives would think of going round via the Causeway, but, braving the terrors of the deep, would cross in the ferryboat."

To call the ferryman intending passengers made hand signals from the opposite shore.

For many centuries the River Severn was a barrier between England and Wales, travellers from Bristol wishing to go to Chepstow having to make a long detour via Gloucester or use the Old Ferry which operated from **Aust** on the Bristol side to **Beachley.** This is the narrowest point in the estuary, being only 2 miles across, but it could be a very difficult and dangerous crossing because of the Severn Bore, a tidal wave which rushes up the estuary at a speed of ten to twelve miles an hour. It forms above Sharpness and can be as much as nine feet high in the centre of the river. In fact, Mr Groves, who until his death recently, was one of the oldest living ferrymen who had served on the Aust/Beachley Ferry, assured me that there is a greater rise and fall of the tide at Chepstow than practically anywhere else in the world.

Small wonder that there were numerous accidents when this ferry was running, especially in earlier days. But travellers preferred this to taking the long detour via Gloucester when wishing to cross the river from Avon to South Wales.

Ben Brown, who was skipper of the *Severn Queen*, and a ferryman from 1952/66, and is now landlord of the *Fiveealls Inn* at Chepstow, said that some riverside landlords regarded a tide-table and a barometer as pieces of essential equipment. When the tide was high and the wind hostile, the prudent landlord would immediately bung up the drains, fix wooden shutters against the lower part of the doorways and plaster them with mud from the river.

Incidentally, the first Bristol Channel tide-tables were made by a Chepstow printer and the local clockmakers made grandfather clocks which indicated the time of high water.

The Beachley/Aust Passage, once known as the Old Passage, was of great antiquity, although there is no historical evidence of its actual age. There is, however, sufficient justification for believing that it existed before recorded time. Some think that the name, Aust, is derived from Augustus, the seventh century Archbishop of Canterbury who, according to tradition, held a conference here with the Welsh bishops, which would suggest that it was in use in Roman times.

Another important ferry crossing this river was known as the New Passage, from **Chessel Pil to Portskewett**. This was probably of later origin but some sort of service operated at Portskewett in the seventeenth century. It is three to four miles south-west of Chepstow and was the principal entrance into Monmouthshire, now Gwent, from Bristol and the western parts of England. The Passage House was built on the summit of the cliff and was known as the *Black Rock Inn*. The landlord leased the ferry and employed local boatmen.

Doubtless ancient Britons crossed the Severn in their dug-out canoes and coracles, in fact one writer states that there were coracles on the River Wye down to Chepstow Bridge as late as the nineteenth century. They were also in use on some of the Welsh rivers.

Later, sailing vessels were used which, as Christopher Jordan records in his *Severn Enterprise,* provided "an uncertain ferry at the whim of the wind and tide which did not really fit the time schedules of the Royal Mail".

The Severn has always been a difficult crossing. The rise and fall of the tide can be as much as 50 feet in just over four hours, while the current flows as fast as eleven knots in the spring tides.

Daniel Defoe in his *Tour through England and Wales* desribed Aust as "a dirty little village," and "the ferry boats to carry over man and beast so mean that we did not venture the passage."

The actual ferry routes varied slightly, so that at one time people were crossing in peril of their lives, and at another able to make the passage in comparative ease.

As Grahame Farr points out in his book *Chepstow Ships,* sailing craft used on the ferries were not registered. There is, therefore, no description with which to identify them but, he suggests, they were probably beamy and flat bottomed, like the shallower examples among the trows which thronged the estuary. The size of the ferries in use in the early nineteenth century can be gathered from the *Elizabeth*, registered in 1831. Her length was 43 feet 9 inches, breadth 12 feet 10 inches.

About 1820 the Aust/Beachley Ferry (Old Passage) came under Government scrutiny. Two famous engineers of the day, Thomas Telford and Robert Stephenson, were asked to report on the respective merits of the Old and New Passages. Although Telford was professionally daunted by the tide-lift, the currents, the hidden rocks and the shoals, and Stephenson received a drenching baptism of spray while crossing in the mail ferry, the Committee of Enquiry still favoured the Old Passage for development. The ferry rights were, therefore, purchased by a new association which included some Welsh M.Ps and businessmen. They decided to repair road approaches and build long stone piers at Aust and at Beachley. They also proposed that the New Passage

he *Severn Queen* and the *Severn King* approaching on the Aust/Beachley crossing.
Captain W. A. Groves Collection. Western Daily Press photograph

(between Portskewett and Chessel Pil) be closed to ensure that the Old Passage had sufficient custom.

Naturally the lessees of the New Passage resented this, especially as they held important Welsh mail contracts. In December 1825 they introduced a small paddle steam boat, the *Saint Pierre.*

Meanwhile the proposed improvements to the Old Passage were made and, in 1827, the first steamer, the *Worcester,* began to operate. Being larger than the *Saint Pierre,* and having the advantage of the new piers, the Post Office transferred most of the mail coaches to the Old Passage. The loss of the coach business forced the owners of the New Passage to sell their steam boat, although a mail coach did operate across the New Passage until 1835. The ferry was still in operation in 1844 but in that year there was an accident resulting in all on board the ferry being drowned.

The Old Passage was not without its disasters for, in 1837, the *Worcester* was burnt; the next *Worcester* was consequently built of iron.

The opening of the Chepstow railway bridge, in 1854, affected the traffic across the Severn, especially as this resulted in the loss of mail contracts which had been of great financial assistance to the ferries. Yet, strangely enough, it was a new railway line, completed in 1863, which revived the New Passage, although the Old Passage was closed.

With the Severn Tunnel built and in operation by 1887 the Aust/ Beachley (Old Passage) Ferry was not re-opened until 1926, when a motor boat was used for passengers and bicycles.

By 1931 a vehicular ferry was in use, the *Princess Ida.* Built of wood, she was a single screw, diesel-engined boat. During the war she was taken over by the Admiralty and sent to Avonmouth for work against sea mines.

Later, the *Severn Princess,* the *Severn Queen* and the *Severn King* were used and these were still in operation when the Severn Bridge was completed and opened in September 1966. Ben Brown, one of the retired ferrymen whom I met when in Chepstow, said that the average number of cars carried on these ferries was 16 on the *Queen,* and 18 on both the *King* and the *Princess.* Horses and gypsy caravans were also part of the traffic taken across. Ben told me that there were times when there was insufficient water for the ferry to operate. Then one ship was left at Beachley, one at Aust and one on the buoy. Queues of people and cars built up, sometimes waiting for five or six hours.

The D.o.T. Committee recognised the problem when they made their Report in 1948 for, having noted that the nearest alternative route was at a point 35 miles upstream from the ferry site, the report continued—

> "The equipment consists of beam loading vessels plying between sloping piers. At week-ends two vessels are engaged in providing a half-hourly service, but at other times one vessel is employed to afford an hourly

service. A third vessel is available as a reserve. The capacities of the three craft are 20, 17 and 9 cars respectively. The distance of the site from the crossing at Gloucester is such that a large volume of through and local traffic seeks to cross by the ferry. On occasion vehicles have to be left waiting on the approaches. We understand that it is intended to proceed with the construction of a road bridge in the near vicinity of the ferry, and that on completion this bridge will supersede the ferry.

In view of the considerable importance of the crossing we conclude that it is essential that an adequate service should be maintained pending the completion of the bridge. It appears, however, that there will be some navigational difficulty in operating the service after the works of construction of the new bridge have commenced unless protective works are carried out on the Beachley side of the river. Our recommendation is based on the assumption that work upon the Severn Bridge will proceed forthwith. If, however, construction is to be postponed indefinitely we are of opinion that further consideration should be given to the scheme which, we understand, has been submitted for an alternative ferry crossing from a point near the Aust terminal of the existing ferry to a terminal near Blackrock in Monmouthshire.* We recommend that —
1. Suitable works should be carried out at or near the Beachley terminal to permit of the continued operation of the ferry during the construction of the Severn Bridge;

*Now Gwent.

The *Severn Queen* loading at Aust Ferry. *Percy Palmer's collection*

2. A half-hourly service should be maintained throughout the week."

A pamphlet published in 1816 by William Stewart, a local engineer and millwright, tells of a **Bristol to Newport** service of weekly "market boats," which was the only means of communication and conveyance between the two places. The accommodation was uncomfortable, the passage uncertain, being dependent on the carriage of goods. The alternative was to travel by coach which was more expeditious and certain, but expensive, while passengers travelling outside were exposed to weather. This part of the journey was followed by a passage on an open boat subject to the piercing winds of the Severn, until, in 1822, the first regular steam packet service was started, and eventually two steamers ran six days a week all the year round.

Grahame Farr in his *West Country Passenger Steamers* reports that little notice was taken by the local press of the *Charlotte,* the 28-ton **Bristol to Bath Ferry**, which began to make daily trips on the Avon in June 1813, with its 4-horse-powered engine. However, a correspondent wrote—"I have been much pleased by steam being used in inland navigation. I have been more than once up and down the river by the steam boat and cannot conceive any mode of travelling so safe, so commodious, so cheap, or so little exposed to dust and heat of summer. The cabin is large enough for 25 to 30 persons who have the sole privilege of a seat on top of the front cabin and on the forecastle, which is railed round and seated."

During the rebuilding of the Keynsham Bridge the opportunity was taken to overhaul the *Charlotte* and improve both machinery and accommodation resulting in increased speed, passenger comfort and cargo space. The local press remarked on her increased manoeuvrability and stopping ability.

There is mention of a ferry across the Nedd at **Neath** in the twelfth and thirteenth centuries.

In Roman times military or trading vehicles conveyed their goods across the river from **Briton Ferry** to West Wales, while travellers on foot or on horseback shortened their journey by using this ferry. Welsh lords held the rights in Roman times. The crossing was reported as treacherous because of its sandbanks and strong currents. Gerald the Welshman and Archbishop Baldwin were nearly drowned when their boat was caught in these currents when they were on a preaching crusade to get recruits to fight in the Holy War of 1188.

There are many references to smuggling activities here. The proprietress of the inn, Katherine Lloyd, being apprehended for receiving the spoils. She doubtless became involved in this illicit practice because the cellars at the *Ferryboat Inn* were under water when the tide was in and smugglers were able to float their casks into the cellars.

An amusing story is told about a comedian arriving at this ferry. It concerned one Charles Matthews who arrived at the ferry with his horse and

These photographs, circa 1905, show the river crossing at Briton Ferry at low and high tide. The plank walkway used for crossing when the tide was out, was covered by some twenty one feet of water at high tide and the rowing boat ferry was used. The *Ferryboat Inn* seen on the far side of the river, the Swansea side, is not the notorious one used by smugglers. That inn was on the near eastern river bank, the Briton Ferry side. *Cliff Morgan's collection*

found himself unable to cross for want of the few pence required for the toll. A beggar who had previously asked him for alms helped him out of his difficulty by lending him a shilling!

The ferry ceased to function when the bridge over the River Neath was completed at the end of October 1955. Until that time the flat-bottomed boat, which was poled across the river, had become an essential means of transport for school children and those people living in Briton Ferry and working at the Elbe Tinplate Works in Jersey Marine. After their walk to the ferry boat they crossed on the ferry in all weathers and had another walk to the Jersey Marine Road to their place of work. From 1951 the ferry was also used by the workmen who were constructing the bridge.

There were many ancient ferries in Wales. Two at **Swansea** operated over the Tawe; one at Pipe House served the Hafod and Foxhole district, and the other at the entrance of the river catered for the residents of Lower Swansea. One of the oldest hostels in the town, the *Beaufort Arms,* served as the ferry house for the Pipe House Ferry which was about three miles down the river from Wychtree Bridge. The burgesses of Swansea were granted the charter for this ferry in 1165. It became a popular ferry and continued in use until the bridge was built in 1850.

The *Cleddau King* at the Neyland side of the Haven. This ferry service linked Pembroke Dock and Neyland on the Milford Haven side before the Cleddau Bridge was built.
Cliff Morgan's collection

The **Hobbs Point to Neyland Ferry**, Dyfed, was investigated by the Department of Trade in 1948 as a result of which the Committee recommended that a floating landing stage should be provided at Hobbs Point and two new vessels should be put into service. One was to be of larger capacity than the existing vessels for normal use and another smaller boat as a reserve to augment the service at peak hours and in summer. The two existing vessels were expected to become unavailable.

The craft in use at that time consisted of two beam loading steam vessels plying between a floating landing stage at Neyland, on the Milford Haven side, and a sloping pier at Hobbs Point, on the Pembroke Dock side, one to operate the service and the other in reserve, each vessel having a capacity of seven vehicles.

With an estimated population of 14,000 on one side of the waterway and a population of 12,000 on the other side, it was considered there was sufficient traffic to justify the continuance of the ferry, especially with the addition of the tourist population, and the likelihood of an increasing demand. It was suggested that the difficulties of boarding and landing at Hobbs Point possibly caused a certain amount of traffic to make a detour of 28 miles around the Haven.

A D.o.T. Report recommended that a vehicular ferry service should be provided for the ancient **Aberdovey Ferry**, Gwynedd, which linked the north side of the River Dovey with the south side. This was the nearest crossing for road traffic, but the route was often impassable in winter months because of floods. The Committee considered that improved crossing facilities would increase the demand for the ferry.

I was unable to visit many of the Welsh ferries, but Henry Rees Davies has covered most of these in his comprehensive book, *A Review of the Records of the Conway and the Menai Ferries,* in which he gives their history prior to the fifteenth century through to the twentieth century.

Henry III's elder son, Edward I, established the **Abermenai Ferry** to cover the two miles from Caernarvon, Gwynedd, to the southernmost tip of Newborough Warren, Anglesey.

No recommendations were made by the D.o.T. Committee for the conversion of two passenger ferries to carry vehicular traffic across the **Menai Straits**, since no representations had been received. The ferries concerned were the **Caernarvon and Port Dinorwic/Moelydon.**

The earliest mention of the **Conway Ferry** was in 1188, and during the years following 1247, Henry III drew revenue from this ferry when he was established east of the Conway River with his strong castle at Degannwy.

The **Tal-y-Cafn Ferry** was held in association with the Conway Ferry for over two hundred and fifty years. In his *A Review of the Records of the Conway*

The monks operate their own ferry from here, Caldy Island, to Tenby, Dyfed. The pier consists of sunken iron barges filled with concrete. *Cliff Morgan's Collection*

and the Menai Ferries, Henry Rees Davies writes that a resident in the locality who frequently crossed is reported to have said that "the large flat ferry-boat, which the ferryman used to wind across by means of a chain passing round a winch, was awkward to handle on the ebb tide when the river was in flood. The stream carried it down to the extreme limit of the chain's scope and there was difficulty in working it up again to its landing place upon the opposite shore. There were also considerable difficulties in landing and embarking vehicles, when the level of the water was low."

When the Tal-y-Cafn Bridge was opened, on 9th October 1897, as part of the ceremony the old ferry boat, which had been moored to the bridge, was cast adrift.

One of the most ancient and interesting group of ferries is that which crossed the **Mersey**, serving the Birkenhead/Wallasey/Liverpool area. The rights of ferry across the Mersey have origins that are centuries old. The river was a formidable obstacle to communication between these places, being considered too wide, too swift and too deep to be bridged and hazardous for small craft.

In his book—*The Mersey Estuary*—John Allison, Chairman of the Liverpool and District Branch of the Geographical Association, speaks of the Mersey as a much greater physical barrier than the Thames in London, with the result that no settlement had developed on the Wirral facing the young port of Liverpool. He goes on to suggest, however, that a crossing of some sort may have existed before the time of the Doomsday survey because the Lord of Wallasey was also the Lord of Kirkdale on the opposite bank.

Ferries have been operated from various points of the Mersey. From the most seaward point there was the New Brighton Ferry which was closed in 1971 with the consent of the Secretary of State, under Wallasey Corporation Act of 1852. Egremont Ferry was closed in 1941, the Rock Ferry was abandoned in 1939 and the New Ferry in 1922. The Eastham Ferry, with vessels given names of precious stones such as *Pearl* and *Ruby*, took an hour to cross sailing against the tide. It was closed at the turn of the century.

The craft used in the early days across the Wallasey Pool, say E. C. Woods and P. C. Brown, authors of a paper, *The Rise and Progress of Wallasey*, prepared for the Wallasey Corporation, "appear to have been single masted, little larger than the life-boats now carried on the stern of their successors. Later, two-masted boats, or grabs were used. Landing was a simple matter, passengers wading ashore or being carried through the shallows by the boatmen. A primitive gangway is described as consisting of a plank supported on two large wheels. The price of a saddle horse in this part of the world was then materially affected by its ability to jump out of a ferry boat cleanly and land its rider safely on terra firma! The smaller boats, with one mast each, were preferred to the larger with two as they were considered handier and could land in shallower water besides being capable of being rowed in calm or contrary winds, and were equally safe." There is a 30 foot rise and fall of the tide in Liverpool which is the reason for a floating landing stage being provided in more recent years.

A century ago there were six ferries operating from the borough of Birkenhead to the opposite shores, the oldest and most important being the Woodside Ferry. The Charter for this ferry was granted to the Monks of Birkenhead Priory by Edward III in 1330. Being a peninsula jutting into the Mersey estuary, Woodside was a good embarkation point, for not only did it command the shortest river crossing, but it had a narrow shelving and rocky foreshore as a firm foundation for a primitive quay.

The service on Monks Ferry was inaugurated illegally in 1838 and was, in the same year, the subject of a successful legal action by the Woodside Ferry Company for the infringement of the ancient rights of the Woodside Ferry. The closure of Monks Ferry, and the purchase of its property two years later by the Birkenhead and Chester Railway Company, which, by this time, had acquired the controlling interest in the lease of Woodside Ferry, was followed, in 1842, by its resale to the Birkenhead Commissioners on condition that consent be given to the construction of a tunnel from Grange Lane Station to Monks Ferry. Three years later the ferry was reopened for the exclusive use of railway passengers. In 1878 the ferry was closed again and the railway passenger traffic diverted to Woodside Ferry and to the newly constructed Woodside railway terminus.

After passing through many different hands throughout the years, Mersey

The Liverpool Landing Stage used by the Mersey Ferries and the daily passenger and car ferry service to the Isle of Man. The enclosed dock on the right of the stage is the terminal for the nightly Belfast ferry. Today this one hundred year old stage, a wooden structure floating on steel pontoons, has been replaced by a new one of cellular concrete units which rise and fall with the tide. *The Mersey Docks and Harbour Company*

Passenger Transport Executive, formed in 1969, was given the responsibility for operating the Mersey ferries.

The Birkenhead Ferry was inaugurated about 1820. It was designed to meet the needs of the newly-built *Birkenhead Hotel* located at the southern corner of the Woodside front and was equipped with a slip and a small dock which at first gave it the best landing facilities of any of the ferries. The grounds of the hotel lay near the slip.

For the first twenty years of its existence it enjoyed a period of prosperity due to the hotel being an important social centre and coach terminus, but with the opening of the Chester railway and the rapid decline of the coaching traffic in 1840, the ferry was closed and the property purchased by the Corporation of Liverpool.

A number of ferries in the townships south of Birkenhead were established during the sixteenth to eighteenth centuries, their actual origin being obscure, although doubtless they received some impetus from the coaching traffic which developed in the late eighteenth century between the Mersey shores and Chester and Parkgate. Despite this, however, the Wirral was an isolated region even at the beginning of the nineteenth century, few caring to undertake the river crossing except under pressure of business or of necessity.

Seacombe ferry, Woodside's nearest rival, is the only ferry other than Woodside which exists today providing a full day time service. No vehicles were carried after 1947 and the night service ceased in 1962, six years after the Woodside night service ended. A shore-based radar station was installed at Seacombe Ferry in 1946/7 as a navigational aid to the ferry.

Seacombe was located virtually on an island, whereas Woodside was open to practically the whole of the Wirral. In 1586 the Seacombe Ferry silted up and a passage and boat were set up at Tranmere. This appears to have been a temporary measure, taken at a particular time in the ferry's history.

In 1821 only sailing boats were in use on the ancient ferry at Seacombe, but in 1822 the first passenger service was inaugurated by the wooden paddler *Seacombe*, although no facilities were provided for horse-drawn vehicles until 1880.

A few years after 1835 a new stone slip for Seacombe steamers was launched at the south end of Prince's Dock. It was 450 feet long and 15 feet wide, with an incline of 1 in 20. About twenty years later the increasing number of passengers made it necessary to widen the stage and slip to 21 feet.

Cuthbert Woods, in his *History of the Wallasey Luggage Boats*, writes of a lady moving house from Everton to Seacombe. Her recollections of her experience on the ferry show the conditions prevailing there at that time.

> "Our furniture having left Everton at 8 a.m. on a November morning in 1852 did not reach Seacombe until evening, having been round

> Birkenhead and the Half-Penny Bridge (Poulton) was carried in by the cheerful light of a tallow candle jammed against the doorpost."

The author comments,

> "The Mersey ferry services, such as they were, were private ventures, indifferently run and not too efficiently organised. Boats were frail, boatmen reckless and dishonest, crossings infrequent and, in rough weather, dangerous. Few people cared to cross the Mersey except of necessity or for business purposes. Complaints were made that the steamers acted as tugs when opportunity arose, with scant regard for the convenience of passengers. In 1863 the Seacombe Service was purchased from the brothers Colebourn by the Wallasey Commissioners for the community, and by the mid-sixties a luggage-boat service was a feature of cross-river transport. None of the earlier vessels had been built specially for the carriage of goods, livestock and light vehicles, but may have been adapted for such use."

The first vessel to be designed and built as a luggage boat was the iron paddler *Sunflower* in 1879, although the first steam ferry boat on service in the Mersey was the *Etna*, built in 1817. She had two hulls, each 63 feet long on either side of a paddle wheel, her deck 28 feet beam, but J. E. Allison, in his *Mersey Estuary,* notes that neither the *Etna* nor her successors gave much comfort, for "passengers were invariably tossed about and frequently had to choose between being half drowned on deck or half suffocated near the boilers below."

However, in the early 1860's, with the modern saloon and screw steamers, things began to improve and tying up the vessel in a tidal basin, or at a pier or landing slip, was a great advance on the earlier beach landing. These landing slips developed in size and design with the progression of years until the modern floating stage of today.

By 1840 all Merseyside ferries had steam boats. In addition to having their distinctive funnel markings, or destination boards, they were distinguished by letters or other devices at the mastheads—"W" for Woodside, "S" for Seacombe, a ball for Birkenhead, a star for Rock Ferry and a locomotive for the rail ferry.

Diesel propulsion was introduced on the Seacombe ferry service in 1951 with the diesel electric cruise vessel *Royal Iris*, followed in the same year by *M.V. Leasowe* and *M.V. Egremont* in 1952.

Woodside is the landing stage for Birkenhead. It was originally known as Birkenhead Ferry. It has survived despite the diversion of the bulk of the vehicular and heavy goods traffic and the consequent loss of revenue following the opening of the Mersey Rail Tunnel in 1886, and the road tunnel in 1934 between Birkenhead and Liverpool.

The Merseyside Passenger Transport Executive claim that they maintain regular and frequent services in all tides and weather and that no fatal accident has occurred since they took over the service. They add that experts praise the skill with which the vessels are manoeuvered in a difficult estuary. Radar assists the vessels across the river in mist and fog and avoids the necessity for cessation of service in such weather.

Two new motor vessels came into service in 1960 and a third in 1962 to replace the steam vessels. These are 142 feet in length and 39 feet in breadth. They are powered by two diesel engines and are each authorised to carry approximately 1,200 passengers. They are claimed to be as modern in design as any vessel.

In spite of this, however, the ferry which dates back more than six hundred years, was losing £1 million a year in 1977 with passengers dwindling to between 11,000 and 12,000 a day, only a sixth of the total of twenty years ago.

The ferries had prospered with the growth of ports and cities in the Estuary; their most prosperous period being between 1880 and 1910. 10,500,000 passengers used Seacombe Ferry during 1955/56, but it made a profit of only £2,000. Twenty years later, when fewer than two million people were using the service, the loss was £477,000: Woodside Ferry lost £60,000 in 1955/56 when it carried 8 million passengers, and with only 1½ million passengers carried in 1975/76 the Transport Executive authority lost £418,000. These reductions in traffic and consequent loss of revenue were, as stated earlier, caused by the opening of the rail and road tunnels, while the new Merseyside railway loop line, giving the largest underground rail link outside London, and the most modern in Europe, was expected to have a still greater effect on the Woodside Ferry, which apparently proved to be the case.

Petitions have been signed against the threatened closing of the ferry, which is still very important to many workpeople, and the Woodside Ferry has been reprieved, at any rate for the present. It remains to be seen how long it will survive.

As a conclusion to this part of the Mersey ferry story, and as an indication of the impression the ferry scene made on these who crossed in the red-funnelled boats from Birkenhead to Liverpool, I quote from an article by a friend who was a resident there but is now living in Sussex:-

> "In the days before the Mersey Tunnel was built, and before everyone had a little tin box on wheels to ride in, it was a fascinating sight to watch the business crowds pacing slowing round the ferry boat decks, deep in conversation. The bowler-hatted brigade and their secretaries, the shop girls and the shipping clerks, kept up their slow march round the *Royal Iris* and the *Royal Daffodil*. The 'Royal' prefix had been granted to

commemorate the gallant performance of the previous *Iris* and *Daffodil* at Zeebrugge and the battle-scarred funnel was preserved at one of the ferries as proof of its gallantry . . .

The red-funnelled ferry boats crossed to Birkenhead, which was a dock town and regarded by us as a rather shabby relation, accepted on sufferance. There were two destinations for the white-funnelled boats. The business people, and all those in a hurry, crossed to Seacombe, from whence busy yellow buses scurried in every direction. Those with more leisure savoured the longer voyage to New Brighton. The long promenade extended the whole way, and all the dear familiar landmarks unrolled like a scroll as one passed . . .

The ferry ended its journey at New Brighton pier where the one-legged diver who later inspired Tommy Handley's 'Don't forget the diver' was a familiar sight.

Halfway along the promenade there was a damaged pier where the ferry used to stop, and nearby was Mother Redcap's—an old 16th century house."

The *Royal Daffodil* — a Mersey Ferry. *R. Bird*

CHAPTER TWO

Crossing the Waters

The Tyne down to the Thames

A PASSENGER ferry across the River Tyne existed at least from the fourteenth century for there are references to it in early documents. By April 1585, and probably much earlier, it had been adapted for horses as well as passenger traffic, for, in the evidence given concerning a Scotsman arrested at Tynemouth on suspicion of treason, it was mentioned that he came to "see the horse boates on Shields."

When the Jacobite Rebellion began, in 1715, the ferry was seized by the commander of the Royal troops who took away the boats for three days to prevent possible use by the rebels.

There seems to have been little attempt to extend or improve the ferry service across the Tyne over the following years. In the early part of the nineteenth century, there was no convenient means of conveyance between North Shields and South Shields and with an increasing population it was important that something should be done.

The question of building a suspension bridge came under discussion from 1824 to 1826, but owing to the depressed state of the money market the idea was dropped.

In 1827 a private company, the North and South Shields Ferry Company, was formed with the intention of adapting steam boats to work the ferries, not only for passengers but for the conveyance of carriages, horses, cattle and merchandise between **North and South Shields**. An Act was passed to establish a ferry and provide adequate access roads to it.

A maximum scale of tolls was fixed and it was further enacted that no other vessel of four tons and upwards should be allowed to be set up in competition with it within a specified area either side of it. This led to the Dean and Chapter claiming an ancient ferry right between the two towns. An agreement between the two parties was reached whereby the Dean and Chapter sold their ferry rights to the new company in consideration of the payment of one-fifteenth of the annual profits, while the Duke of Northumberland's claim of 6s. 8d. per annum for the landing rights of the old ferry on the north side of the river was admitted.

White and Hodgson of South Shields built this version of the ferry *Durham* which was sunk by a German bomb in 1942. *South Tyneside Public Libraries and Museums*

When the North and South Shields Ferry Company was formally constituted, in 1829, to run the ferry across the Tyne it spent £10,415 in building boats, acquiring and preparing landings, and establishing the ferries. But things did not get off to a good start for the boats originally used proved useless and had to be replaced. One of the two original ferry boats used was the *Durham*. She was described as a veritable curiosity of naval architecture being a "double-hulled wooden steamer, propelled by one gigantic clumsy paddle wheel in the centre. Her twin hulls were joined by an iron stanchion and the craft looked like a floating dock. The ponderous gangway had to be raised and lowered by a hand winch, an arrangement which did not conduce to the safety of the passengers, nor to the improved morale of the employees, for sometimes the apparatus refused to work."*

In addition to passengers she was capable of carrying four carts and took twenty minutes to make the journey against a spring tide.

Her replacement, the first *Northumbria*, though of a different type and having only a single hull, was "lacking so seriously in stability that a bogie, heavily laden with chains, had to be run on rails from side to side, an action

**Borough of South Shields from the Earliest Period to the Close of the Nineteenth Century.* G. B. Hodgson.

required to maintain her proper balance. When she listed she took in water copiously."* At low tide she could not land passengers except by the use of rowing boats. Ferries were irregular, often being delayed by the tide, with passengers having a two hour wait. By the time the boat was able to leave the big crowd which had collected made a rush for it.

There was also the problem of the ferry grounding on the sand in the middle part of the harbour where it would remain fast for a couple of hours.

It is not surprising, therefore, that the ferry company lost money in its early years and when it did become profitable it was threatened by competition from passenger steamers crossing the Tyne with different ports of call. Eventually, after many vicissitudes, the Tyne Commisioners took over the ferry on 1st May 1863 and retained the responsibility for its operation until, in 1972, they passed it over to the Tyneside Passenger Transport Executive, the then owners of the bus services in Newcastle and South Shields. They agreed to run a passenger only service if this could be done at very much less cost. The alternative was no ferry service at all.

It was not until May 1972 that the Tyneside Passenger Transport Executive started its New Shields Ferry Time and Fare Table. This stated that a new vessel would operate a 20 minute service during the peak period compared with the 30 minute service previously run by the Commissioners with the *Northumbria* which was now worn out after forty years service, and had latterly been losing its owners £1,000 a week.

Fares were to be 10p for adults, 5p for children and 3p for a bicycle or pram.

Still there were delays, the *Freda Cunningham,* named after the wife of the Chairman, suffered delays in completion due to minor technical problems and at the launching which also had to be delayed. This slowed down crew training. Necessary alteration to the North Shields landing stage could not be carried out until the *Northumbria* went out of service.

The *Freda Cunningham* was a comparatively small vessel, though equipped with radar. It was planned to keep down building and running costs. The number of foot passengers had fallen from one and a half million in 1967 to under half a million in 1971. A survey made during the previous year had shown that only five sailings a day carried over 100 passengers and on a 30 minute service, therefore a more frequent service, with a smaller boat, appeared both adequate and cheaper. It was pointed out that any losses on the new service would have to be met by ratepayers.

Later the *Shieldsman* was added to the service. The need to turn about for the return crossing was obviated by her construction which allowed disembarkation from either end.

The Voith Schneider propellers† installed gave her many advantages in operation. The ramps, six and a half feet wide, were designed to allow

**Borough of South Shields from the Earliest Period to the Close of the Nineteenth Century.* G. B. Hodgson.

†These have variable pitch blades, giving greater manoeuvrability including that of moving the vessel sideways.

passengers to disembark easily and quickly, whether handling wheelchairs, perambulators or cycles and no matter what the weather.

There were other ferries running on the Tyne. Starting at five o'clock each weekday morning, the Tyne Passenger Boat Company ran a regular service of steamers, known as the Red Star Line, between **Shields and Newcastle.** This began to function on 1st September 1859. A Parliamentry Bill of 1862 empowered the Company to function as the Tyne General Ferry Company and their steamer paddle boats operated over the full navigable length of the Tyne—from Tynemouth piers to Blaydon, a distance of approximately 20 miles, calling at 26 landings on both the north and south banks.

A past employee who served his apprenticeship on these boats recalled that at one time there were 21 vessels engaged in this service, which catered for the many employees of the shipyards and other industries. Some of these boats were certified to carry as many as 600 passengers. Merchandise also was carried on the ferries. At the beginning of the twentieth century transport by land, which was much quicker and not so much affected by weather conditions, caused a considerable reduction in river traffic with the result that, in 1907, the company ceased to operate and went into liquidation.

Although the ferry was no longer financially viable, its closure was very inconvenient for people who had been accustomed to travel on these boats to and from their places of work. However, for many years Hawthorn and Leslie, one of the large shipbuilding firms at Hebburn, had maintained their own service for the convenience of their work force. Starting with rowing boats they were now using two steam boats, each capable of carrying 272 passengers. The cessation of the Tyne General Ferry Company made it necessary for the Hebburn Shipbuilding Company to cater for their employees who had been using the other company's crossing from Walker to Hebburn and back, and they agreed to purchase two additional steam boats to maintain this extra passage. These became so popular not only with workpeople but also the general public, that in 1939 the shipbuilding company, faced with the replacement of the old steam ferry boats, gave notice of their intention to close the service.

A group of Tyneside firms therefore joined the shipping company in forming the Mid Tyne Ferries Company, purchasing two new diesel boats to replace the outworn steam vessels previously in use. Apart from operating advantages these diesel-engined boats gave a large area of clear deck space, each ferry being licensed to carry on deck 314 passengers. The two vessels were very successful and in 1948 it was decided to add a third diesel-driven boat with similar dimensions.

An article in *Crossley Chronicles,* dated May 1950, claims that these ferries had been running every day including Sundays and holidays, from 6.30 a.m.

until 10.30 p.m. They then conveyed about 1½ million passengers annually and sometimes exceeded 7,000 a day during the war years.

With only one old and narrow bridge spanning the River Ouse until the Selby Bridge was satisfactorily completed in 1792, there must have been an exceptional number of ferries crossing and recrossing this river. One writer puts it at over a score and Duckham, in his book *The Yorkshire Ouse,* actually names as many as seventeen such ferries. Most of them have long since passed into obscurity, as has the **Whitgift Ferry**, though it was once the most important of those on the Lower Ouse. Charles I must have used it when he moved south from York to Nottingham, in 1642. The only reminder of this is the inn, once the old ferry house.

The origins of **Skeldergate and Lendal Ferries** at York are rather obscure but by Tudor times they were in the possession of the City Corporation who normally let them to the highest bidder. This applied as recently as 1850, for an order by the Town Clerk appeared in the *York Gazette* in March that year reading:-

> "Lot 2. The ferry and passage over the River Ouse between Skeldergate Postern and the New Walk, and all the profits thereto belonging together with the ferryman's house near thereto."

These ferries were worked successfully until the growth of the population made it necessary for bridges to be built to replace them. In 1862 passengers using the Lendal Ferry numbered 293,460. The bridge at Lendal was opened at the beginning of the next year, 1863.

About twelve years prior to the erection of the Skeldergate Bridge a certain John Leeman became ferryman of the Lendal Ferry. As he was about to lose his occupation when the bridge was opened a public subscription was raised for him and on 13th May 1863 he was presented with a horse and cart which cost £25, and with £15 in cash.

Between York and Selby there were ferries at **Bishopsthorpe, Naburn, Acaster** and **Cawood.**

The Benedictine Abbey at **Selby** was founded in 1069 and it is most probable that the monks established the ferry there during that century, the river crossing being the link between the East and West Ridings. Selby was then the second largest town on the Ouse. The ferry ran continuously until 1792 by which time the Selby Canal had been opened bringing fresh trade to the Ouse and Selby in particular, and, incidentally creating demands for a bridge across the river. Following the Dissolution of the Monasteries the ferry and ferryboat of Selby had, like many others, been seized by the Crown and the rights granted to Sir Ralph Sadler of Middlesex, who now found himself having the rights of a profitable undertaking worth a good deal of compensation in the event of it being replaced by a bridge.

The *Lincoln Castle* on the Humber. Although now retired the *Lincoln Castle* was Britain's last coal-fired paddle-steamer still in ferry service in 1977. *Captain Harvey*

To test the claims of the owner of the Selby Ferry about the volume of traffic on the ferry a census was taken of its use during a given month. The result showed the following figures: persons on foot—8,743; persons with horses—3,052; led horses—211; oxen—127; hogs—66; sheep—2,248; coaches—1; chaises—15; single-horse chaises—9; waggons—3; carts—16.

The jury decided in favour of a bridge, but the ferry owner had arranged matters to his advantage for not only was he compensated for the loss of the ferry but he had acquired a financial interest in the bridge building.

When Selby ceased functioning, in 1791, the passage at **Booth** became the premier Ouse ferry. Being on the direct route from Hull and with the growth of Goole it became increasingly important. It was the longest surviving ferry on this river, only ceasing when the steel swing Boothferry Bridge was opened in 1929. The ferry had been leased out to different people; the best known lessees were the Wells family, who ran a large coaching establishment at the inn and ferryhouse. John Wells had a share in several Goole ships.

The Humber estuary was once part of the counties of Yorkshire and Lincolnshire but in April 1974 became part of the new county of Humberside. It is formed by the junction of the rivers Ouse and Trent and carries the waters of these and other rivers, such as the Derwent and the Calder, to the North Sea. Regular crossings of the Humber have been made since well before the Romans came to Britain. Commercial exploitation over the intervening years has involved a multiplicity of routes, enterprises and technologies.

The **Stoneferry and Drypool Ferry** was in use in the thirteenth century and a charter for a new ferry, North Ferry, was granted to the Burgesses of Kingston upon Hull, the full official name of the city, at the end of that century. This ferry was replaced by a bridge in 1541.

In August 1315 the **Hull to Barton Ferry** was established, charging tolls for the King's use on pedestrians, horsemen, carts and animals. It became known as the South Ferry. The Town Council complained to the King in 1393 that the Barton ferryman was interfering with the ferry from Hull. He was ordered at once to desist. The ferry comprised a sailing ship and a cog* or small boat.

The efficiency of the ferry was frequently criticised during the seventeenth century and the lease often changed hands. The rent rose from £30 to £200, this latter figure included the rent of the lessee's house at South End. There was friction between the lessee and private boatmen who took passengers to the Barton side, and rivalry between the crews.

Throughout the century safeguards for the better running of the ferry were written into tenants' leases; from 1640 they were required to provide six men to man the vessels.

In 1673 the Corporation proposed that a small crane should be installed at the Horse Staith to remove coaches from the sailing ship. The Hull Guide of

*Small sailing craft used on the Humber and River Ouse.

1806 states that this service was carried on "by not less than four large boats of 45 tons burthen and several smaller ones which will take 15 to 25 persons each." These passenger vessels sometimes carried as many as 300 people in a day, especially on Sunday afternoons. The horse boats' capacity was four four-wheeled carriages, the same number of gigs and up to 50 horses.

The Guide also notes that boats made the passage in 40 or 50 minutes, seldom longer than two hours and, on an average, did not exceed one hour and twenty minutes. The small boats were often hired by people who arrived too late for the hoy.*

By 1801 traffic in and out of the harbour at Hull had made it necessary to build a dock, improve the market place and build a wide road to the dock; also an enlarged landing place for the ferry boats was provided. By 1833 ferries from Hull were timed to catch coaches from Gainsborough to Retford, Sheffield and Newark, and to London, favourable circumstances permitting. Barton Ferry was also a link for London coaches. "Favourable circumstances" doubtless referred to tides, for ferries from Hull were subject to the state of the tide. This ferry link with coach services reduced the price of the journey compared with that of passengers who had to travel all the way by coach. However, with the coming of the river steamer and increasing rail services, coaching traffic lessened and finally ceased.

The *Caledonia*, a paddle sloop, was the first steamer which appeared on the Humber. She commenced service between Hull and Gainsborough in 1814. Other steamers soon followed trading to Selby and other places, and linking up with coach routes to the advantage of both services.

At that time regional railway companies were in operation and, in 1845, the Great Grimsby and Sheffield Junction Railway became interested in the purchase of this ferry. They bargained with the owners who at first remained firm in their original terms of £11,800, the ferry having a net annual value of £420, but later agreed to accept the original offer of the Railway Company's Committee, the negotiating body, of £10,000. Following this an advertisment appeared in the *Sheffield and Rotherham Independent*, reading:

> "The directors (of the GG & SJ) have also to announce that they have, on their own individual responsibility, purchased from the proprietors, the whole of their valuable property and privileges in the ferries from New Holland and Barrow to Hull, with land, and buildings at both landing stages, deeming it most important to the success of the undertaking that the property at once be secured by them, and essential to the future working of the Railway, that the arrangements for the Ferry should be under their control."

The Provisional Committee which had been appointed to negotiate the deal included some of the directors of the railway company who acted as

*A small coastal vessel of up to 60 tons approximately, usually fore- and aft-rigged.

In 1957 Father Neptune, with the co-operation of the ferrymen, held his court during a school cruise on the Humberside Ferry, *Tattersall Castle*. Those presented at court were given a special certificate. *Hull Daily Mail*

guarantors. Apparently it was they, the Provisional Committee, who had purchased the ferry in trust until the railway company had obtained the necessary Act of Parliament.

But the Railway Company had second thoughts and the ferry became the private concern of the 14 members of the Committee. The irony was that, about eight months later, the railway decided they must have the ferry and agreed to pay the then owners £21,000! Thus the committee originally appointed by the railway, which included some railway directors, made a profit of £11,000 in the nine months in which they had held the ferry, a profit of over 100 per cent.

Many stories have been told about each of these Humber ferries, but it was the Sealink Humber Ferry service, operating between Hull and New Holland which became the most important and is still operating, in spite of the operator's claim that it is losing money. A service from New Holland was started by Thomas Dent in the early years of the nineteenth century. He built a cottage and a large shed where he kept a boat. Journalists of that time claimed it to be a cloak for smuggling activities from New Holland which was then an isolated creek lending itself to such practices.

In 1825 New Holland Ferry developed from its humble beginnings. A Barton man purchased some land near that owned by Dent and formed a company known as New Holland Proprietors, which purchased a small boat and, in 1826, improved hotel facilities by building the *Yarborough Arms,* now renamed the *Lincoln Castle*. The roads to and from New Holland were improved and the London stage coach route was transferred from Barton.

About 1832 a steam ferry, the *Magna Charta*, was brought into service running from New Holland to Hull, completing three round trips per day with an extra one on market days.

When the railway acquired the ownership of this ferry, a pier was built at New Holland. It was over a quarter of a mile long with a rail terminus at the riverside end. John Fowler, who later designed the Forth Bridge, created it.

Two second-hand paddle steamers, the *Queen* and the *Prince of Wales,* joined the *Magna Charta,* and over the next few years the *Manchester, Sheffield, Royal Albion, Liverpool* and *Doncaster* came into service, the last two being built in Hull in 1855 and 1856. At the same time the Railway Company agreed to make an annual payment of £40 for the use of Victoria Pier as a landing berth for their ferries. Prior to that, in 1869, the floating pontoon at New Holland pier was damaged and sunk in a violent storm. It was replaced by a slipway. Other vessels were added until, during the First World War, three of the ferries were requisitioned by the Admiralty and converted into seaplane carriers.

The increasing popularity of motor cars, and the difficulties of transporting them on the ferries, made it necessary to lift them on and off by crane until an agreement was reached to improve the terminal facilities at Hull and New Holland. This involved the installation of floating pontoons 150 feet long and 50 feet wide, with connecting hinged and covered bridges. These are still in use, the bridges being 23 feet wide with a central roadway, ten feet wide, for vehicles. At high water the bridges are approximately level, whilst at low water they have a maximum gradient of 1 in 9. The railway company agreed to collect, on behalf of the Corporation, the tolls from passengers and vehicles using the Victoria Pier.

The improvements were completed in 1934 and two new ferries, the *Tattershall Castle* and the *Wingfield Castle*, two coal burning paddle steamers, came into service. They were designed to cope effectively with the increasing car traffic. On 1st January 1948 the multiplicity of railway companies in Britain were nationalised and are known today as British Rail whilst ferry elements now form part of the railway's Sealink organisation.

The *Tattershall Castle* was the first paddle steamer to be fitted with radar. This was in 1948. But fog is not the only hazard to navigation on the Humber; the other is the lack of a direct navigable channel between Hull and New Holland. The large tidal rise and fall means that, at low tide, shoaling in the centre of the river makes it difficult, and at times impossible, for the ferries to negotiate a crossing. At low spring tides a sandbank, running down the middle of the river, actually emerges above water level. Ferries have been known to be grounded on this in attempting to cross it rather than make the more usual course change to find the navigable channel. This can extend the passage time from the usual twenty minutes to forty minutes or more.

In 1941 the *Lincoln Castle* made the third vessel operating the ferry. She was built specifically for the Humber ferry service and operated for nearly forty years. In March 1978 it was announced that she was to be retired. She was Britain's last coal-fired paddle steamer still in use and the sole survivor of over a century of steam paddlers working on the Humber.

The *Wingfield Castle* and the *Tattershall Castle* were replaced by the *Farringford*, a diesel-driven paddle boat, which was transferred from the Isle of Wight service in 1974. Previously bow- and stern-loading, she was altered to side loading because of the slipway on the Humber Ferry. This vessel was capable of carrying twice as many cars as the displaced ferries.

The *Lincoln Castle,* being less affected by low tides than the *Farringford*, with its greater draught, had usually run the train-connected sailings in order to maintain rail connections in low water conditions.

A few years ago 750,000 passengers, over 100,000 cars and vans, and over 150,000 parcels were carried on the New Holland Ferry. The *Lincoln Castle* was capable of carrying 900 passengers and 18 to 20 vehicles, and the

The Ferry at Martham, Norfolk, where a large pontoon could be floated in position between two earthen ramps when required. It completely blocked the narrow river but cattle and carts could be driven straight across. *R. Malster*

Farringford 500 passengers and up to 36 vehicles. The peak service from New Holland to Hull is between 7 and 10 a.m., while on the return to New Holland the peak for passengers is from 4 to 6.30 p.m.

When I crossed on the *Lincoln Castle,* in the summer of 1977, Mr Fisher told me that the average time taken to discharge and load was 20 minutes, but under ideal conditions it could be done in less. He also said that 1,000 passengers a day were using the ferry.

This vessel could operate at very low water taking continuous soundings at slow speed. The average speed was eight and a half to nine knots but, with the tide against the vessel, speed decreased to six knots.

The opening of the M62 motorway and the widening of the A63 considerably improved road communications and this had an adverse affect on the ferry. In 1980 the Humber Suspension Bridge is due to be opened and this event could well signal the end of the ferry service.

Apart from the almost completed bridge at Hessle, this Hull to New Holland Ferry is the only link between the North and South Bank of the Humber. Without this, and until the bridge is completed, the route from Hull to the south would involve travellers going north to Doncaster to catch the train. Many users feel that, with the bridge set so far from the ferry—which lands its users at a point where there is a good bus service into the centre of Hull—and the high tolls proposed for using the bridge, the ferry is still an essential means of crossing the river, as it has been for about a hundred and fifty years.

Planners studied the problems of having a ferry and a bridge. But for the County to run the ferry without vehicles would have cost £100,000 in 1975. Large sums of money would have had to be spent on getting the boats through the marine equivalent of the M.o.T. test and a staff totalling more than seventy would have had to be employed.

The use of hovercraft has been discussed but this was not considered feasible. The planners say that the ferry is among the most expensive in Europe and bus and rail links, with a new interchange at Barton-on-Humber, could take its place at much less cost. But most people have a soft spot for a tradition going back beyond 1832, when the New Holland steamer service began, to pre-Roman times. However, planners wonder what people will say when they see the costs of keeping the ferry as a passenger service, or even as a mobile museum, which has been the use to which other obsolete ferry boats have been put when they have gone out of service.

A very ancient ferry served the small village of Weel, where there were only a hundred inhabitants. This passage crossed the Hull River connecting **Weel with Beverley**. It was maintained by the tenant of the *Nag's Head* public house. On a number of occasions the ferry sank, but there were, apparently, no casualties, the main concern being the cost of retrieving the flat-bottomed boat from the river. In 1936 the cost of that operation was £75. On another occasion, in 1942, when the Home Guard, in an excess of enthusiasm, marched on to the pontoon it sank completely and the cost of pulling it out was £128. In 1945 it again sank and blocked the river for a short time. On this occasion divers had to be employed but we are not told the cost of this recovery. Nevertheless objections were raised when it was proposed to replace the ferry by a footbridge. On 18th February 1949, the pontoon bridge was swept aside by high water and was lying on the bank of the river while workmen from Beverley Shipyard ferried themselves across the river in a small boat.

From an inn on the northern bank of the Ouse a horse omnibus connected the **Howden Dyke Ferry** with the town of Howden until the 1870's.

The last ferry boat was in the form of a large flat-decked barge, which carried motor vehicles. There are few references to it but it must have remained in commission until after the First World War.

Wintringham Haven to Brough and **Barton to Hessle** were two of the shortest crossings on the Humber, the former being the older of the two.

The Hessle Ferry was active in the fourteenth century with a sailing ship and a cog or small boat. Following complaints of extortionate tolls being charged, it was ordered that dues of a halfpenny for a pedestrian and a penny for a horseman should be charged. The opening of the Hull Selby Railway in 1840 increased the traffic between Barton and Hessle, the crossing being shorter than that between Hull and New Holland, so the Hessle ferry owners timed their services to link up with the trains.

The ferry was popular also with cattle drovers coming south from the Vale of York. They preferred this crossing because the livestock were carried in an open boat and were therefore less likely to suffer injury than when transported below decks as they would have been on other ferries.

The service was maintained until the early nineteenth century when it began to wane.

The history of the **King's Lynn to West Lynn** crossing of the Great Ouse in Norfolk goes back to the eleventh century when two crossings are recorded. Although the actual origins are unknown both continued well into the twentieth century. A small motor boat came into service in 1920 on this essential link between the people of West Lynn and those in the main town of King's Lynn on the other side of the river. Like so many ferries the income failed to keep pace with the growth of operational costs so the ferry passed to the Corporation.

The crossing takes only three or four minutes. In 1967 the ferry was closed for an unspecified period while the pier on the western side was repaired. The public complained that it was a long way round by the bridge but the Town Council said that it would have been too costly to keep the ferry operating while the pier was being replaced.

At one period the Corporation ferry crossed the river sixty times a day transporting workers and housewives, the latter claiming that they could take their prams on the ferry but not on the buses. Some, especially during the winter, considered the crossing hazardous but the great majority considered that it was an amenity.

There were horse ferries at **Runham Swim** and **Cantley Swim** in Norfolk, the name doubtless given to the ferries because herds of cattle were made to swim across the river. At Cantley the ferry boat operated only for the benefit of the workers at the sugar beet factory.

Robert Malster, in *Wherries and Waterways,* 1971, records that Broads horse-ferries were large wooden pontoons hauled across the river by chains passing over wheels fitted to the railing of the pontoon. These were used at **Reedham,** Cantley, **Buckenham** and **Surlingham**. He adds that a variation at **Martham** was of similar design but floated into position between two earthen ramps when required, entirely blocking the narrow river so that cattle or carts could be driven straight across.

At least three vehicular ferries crossed the 26 mile course of the Yare between **Great Yarmouth** and **Norwich**, Norfolk in earlier times. These were at Reedham, Buckenham and Surlingham. Now only Reedham remains in the heart of the marshes of Broadland.

The reason given for the closures of the other ferries was the high cost of repairing the ferry boats and quay headings compared with the amount of traffic likely to use the ferries. Neither of these crossings was re-opened in spite of the Department of Trade 1948 Report that they were of value. It was recommended that the vehicular ferry services at the two sites be restored. It also recommended that they should be capable of carrying loads of up to three tons and that improved methods of boarding and landing should be provided.

One reader pointed out that a vehicle going from Brundell to Surlingham and returning, a distance of a few hundred yards, must travel a distance of 22 miles, now that the ferry was withdrawn, thus also adding to the congestion on the Norwich—Great Yarmouth road.

Following letters written to the local paper complaining about the ferry service across the Yare, the landlord of the *Ferry House Inn* at Surlingham, who was obliged to maintain the service across the river, stated his point of view in a letter to the *Eastern Daily Press:*

> "In fairness to all concerned I should much appreciate your publishing the following facts:-
>
> 1. The winter time-table schedules the ferryboat to make 15 crossings daily, 30 times there and back, in all weathers, including gales and strong running tides.

The Surlingham Ferry and the *Ferry House*. *R. Malster*

The Buckenham Ferry on the Norfolk Broads. *R. Malster*

2. From the time-table it may be seen that the ferryboat service is available 15¼ hours daily, seven days a week, with the one exception of Wednesday, when the ferry does not run between 9.30 a.m. and 2.30 p.m.
3. To maintain the ferry service in accordance with the time-table one has to be 'on duty' 99¼ hours weekly.
4. The weekly income from the boat ferry is under £2, quite insufficient to pay even one man's wages.
5. The Catering Wages Act 1943 lays down minimum and maximum hours and wages, and holidays with pay, etc. for men employed by licensed catering establishments, which would make it impossible to employ such labour during the winter months.
6. Such a public service as a ferryboat service, should not, in my opinion be dependent upon one private individual. Visits to the doctor have been quoted by one correspondent, and I am in sympathy with the writer of that letter, but it should be borne in mind that the person ferrying them across could also be taken ill, and in such an instance the service could not run at all."

The closure of the Buckenham and Surlingham ferries also resulted in a good deal of press publicity during 1949. One correspondent commented that it was intolerable that Norfolk people should have to remain content indefinitely with communications inferior to those available in the days of horse transport, when all three ferries were in regular use, while in July 1963 an article in the *Eastern Daily Press* posed the question:

"Will Surlingham Ferry, which used to provide the only vehicle crossing of the Yare between Reedham and Norwich, ever run again? Some people still wonder why the 1948 recommendation of the Ministry of Transport Committee was never carried. It was that the ferry should be restored and made capable of taking up to three tons.

It may be recalled that the Norfolk County Council went into the question in 1950, when it was reported that the total cost of repairing the quay on the north bank and both road approaches and of providing a new ferry boat would be £15,000. The owners of the ferry rights, who were the brewers, had offered the rights free to the Council, but a committee decided against it—mainly owing to the cost of road works. Now I hear that improvements are being contemplated to the moorings and the quay headings. With the great increase in road traffic in the past thirteen years the value of a ferry would be much greater. A car travelling from Brundall to Surlingham and back now has to go 22 miles instead of a few hundred yards. There used to be a county road sign in Great Plumstead optimistically indicating 'Surlingham 1½ miles'—a survival of the ferry era."

Walter Rye, in an article dated August 1917, described the scene on the Yare when these two ferries were working:-

"Half a century ago the black hulls and white-painted rails of the great, floating, box-like ferries, with their cargoes of farm waggons, farmers gigs, market carts and the village carrier's cart, were as much a part of the peaceful, rural scene as were the pink sunbonnets of the marshwomen and the felt wide-awake hats of the marshmen, who wore their pale blue or white 'sloops' square cut at the neck with full-length gathered sleeves. On Sundays they turned out in double-breasted moleskin waistcoats with long sleeves and reefer jackets of stout blue cloth with a seafaring smack about the whole rig-out."

However, before the ferry was closed the vehicle ferry boat at Surlingham was so old that the ferryman used to warn his would-be passengers: "If you really want to go across I'll take you, but the old boat's rotten and I don't know whether we'll get there."

The first ferry service at Reedham was established around the fifteenth century. Now it is the only ferry travelling across the rivers of Norfolk; in fact, it is the last working car ferry in the whole of East Anglia. With no bridge over the Yare between Norwich and Great Yarmouth, Reedham is the only place where the river can be crossed with a car, thus saving a 34-mile detour.

Stories exist—many doubtless unfounded—of cargoes of smuggled goods being run across the marshes at Reedham to the old ferry inn, the *Cockatrice*, on the opposite bank of the river. One story claims that the sails of the windmills built along the Yare were set in a certain position when Excise men were waiting at the inn. Seeing this the smugglers sailed on to another inn where the windmill signal informed them that it was safe to land the contraband.

At this ferry, where wooden pontoons are used, Arthur Benn, landlord of the *Ferry Inn*, was one of the last Norfolk horse-ferrymen. The Reedham boat which he operated was overhauled in 1930. When fully loaded with a large lorry and a saloon car it drew between two to three feet. It was a pontoon ferry pulled across by a chain weighing just over a quarter of a ton, manually operated by a crank handle. Arthur Benn was still cranking this ferry across the river, all 20 to 30 tons of dead weight, when he was over seventy years old, sometimes with a strong tide running and a cutting easterly wind coming off the marshes.

Another man who remembered the muscle-aching task of winching the ferry across the Yare is Norman Archer. He took responsibility for operating the ferry when it was in a sorry state, with timbers rotten, winch gears and chains worn. The ferry required 94 turns of the crank handle to get it across the river. Norman's son David worked a shift with his father, operating the ferry from 8 o'clock in the morning until 10 o'clock at night. After nine months of winching the ferry across, the Archers installed a small petrol engine and later fitted a 3½ horse-power diesel engine.

Holiday-makers take their cars across in summer just for the ride. At first the rise and fall of the tide created difficulties in getting cars on and off the ferry, but the Archers overcame this by fitting a double drawbridge system which lines up with the quay regardless of the tide position: as one drawbridge is raised the other is lowered automatically. This speeds up the time of loading vehicles.

The toll for a horse and carriage in 1864 was 2s. 6d. (12.5p). In 1964, for a car and driver it was 3s. 3d., (16.25p); only nine pence (3.75p) more in a hundred years.

The ferry was out of action for three weeks in the bad weather of 1962, when the chains collected so much ice that they floated on the river.

The Department of Trade Report of 1948 considered that the needs of agriculture and the flow of sugar beet to Cantley were regarded as being so important that a bridge should be built. A new bridge was accepted in principle by the Norfolk County Council, but the cost led to the indefinite postponement of the scheme.

Sugar beet came from as far south as Southwold to Cantley, but ever since the factory was built, in 1912, getting it across the Yare had been a difficulty, not for the factory, but for the farmers. They had to pay the extra freight involved by the journey round via Norwich or Yarmouth because the ferry could not take the loaded weight on the outward journey, although the empty lorries did make the return journey on the ferry.

It is claimed that **Horning Ferry** existed in the early part of the thirteenth century but it had ceased to function in 1948, when the D.o.T. Report was made. That document stated that "the site is four miles by water from the nearest road bridge, which is at Wroxham" and that no vehicular ferry was in operation at that time. The Report continued: "The equipment which was last in use was of the pontoon and chain type, manually operated, plying between timber landing stages. The capacity was one vehicle of a maximum weight of two tons. The service was operated on demand during daylight hours."

Although it was felt that there was little or no demand by long distance traffic for a vehicular ferry service, local residents had made representations for the restoration of the facilities formerly available, drawing attention to the tourist and holiday traffic, heavy in the area during summer months, which had made use of the ferry in the past. The Committee noted that the ferry site "lies within the boundaries of the proposed National Park embracing the Broads."

The Reedham Ferry in the early twentieth century when the magnificent trading wherries were very much part of the scenery of the Broads. *R. Malster*

Ferryman R. Dye's late grandfather (left) and Uncle Ernest Dye (centre operating the ferry) on the *Fort St George* to old Caius boat yard ferry, Cambridge in 1920. Grandfather Dye ran the ferry from 8 a.m. to 10 p.m. at an old halfpenny each way.

Cambridgeshire Collection, Cambridgeshire Libraries

They recommended that the vehicular ferry service should be restored; the ferry should be capable of carrying a maximum load of two tons as in the past; and should be provided with suitable boarding and landing devices to ensure the safety of vehicles.

Apparently the service was resumed at some time for the author of the *Companion Guide to East Anglia* records that the ferry ceased to function in 1967.

The ferries at **Great Yarmouth**, across the Yare River, appear to have been established without a licence from the Crown and were the subject of much litigation. Originally the passage of the water was granted by the Admiral of the North Sea Fleet. In 1309 the Corporation let off the ferry at 35s. a year. This was a horse ferry, but when the bridge was constructed, in 1417, the passage was reduced to a pedestrian ferry. Workmen used it to save themselves a twenty minute walk.

A right of ferry over the river at **Gorleston** enabled the Rev. George Anguish to establish a passage there when he was Lord of the Manor in 1834.

This was known as the Lower Ferry, being about a mile down the river from the Upper Ferry. With only one bridge over the Bure from Yarmouth to Wroxham, ferries were essential to those wishing to cross this river.

In the eastern counties the navigation of the River Cam between **Cambridge** and **Clayhithe Ferry** was authorised in 1702.

There were no foot bridges across the Cam sixty years ago and the cost of a trip on the ferry between Midsummer Common and the old Caius boatyard was ½d.

A Cambridge man, writing to the *Cambridge Evening News* in January 1972 says his grandfather and uncle, Ernest Dye, ran the ferry from 8 a.m. until 10 p.m. until it was put on chains. The flat-bottomed vessel was operated by turning a wheel with a wooden handle, rather like the old-fashioned clothes mangle, which moved the chains which were stretched across the river. It was a slow process with only a few people able to cross at one time. Walter Pauley was ferryman in the later part of the time the ferry was running, assisted by his son Ernest. Walter Pauley said that during his forty years of serving he had seen 1¼ million people cross the river with no accidents.

The ferry ran from the *Fort St George* steps to the bottom of Ferry Path. Only three ferrymen had operated the ferry over the fifty years of its existence.

Strangely enough the ferryboat sank, with no passengers aboard, a few months before the bridge was built to replace it, after an attempt had been made to effect repairs. When the foot bridge was built Mr Pauley was reported as saying he "didn't hold with these new fangled bridges!"

The **Southwold/Walberswick** ferry has been operating since the thirteenth century, the franchise being granted to the Lord of the Manor. Originally, as was the case of so many other ferries, an open boat was used. In 1885, however, the River Blythe Company was formed to operate the ferry. They provided a mechanically operated pontoon worked by steam and running on chains across the river. It was capable of carrying three cars or one bus. In summer up to 200 cars a day are said to have crossed on the ferry.

The Company continued to operate until 1942 when it went into liquidation, the Lord of the Manor having refused to renew the lease. From this time a rowing boat ferried people across, vehicular traffic having to cross by the bridge at Blythburgh, which is four miles away by water. Six years later the Department of Trade Committee reported "that the pontoon was no longer in serviceable condition, the slipways had suffered damage and the operation of the ferry had become impracticable because of navigational difficulties attributed to the execution of harbour works in the vicinity." They concluded that "the importance to tourists of the areas which were served by the ferry, and the dependence upon Southwold of the local community in the Walberswick area are such as to justify the restoration of some means whereby vehicular traffic may cross the river at this point." Their recommendation was

Horse and passenger ferries at Chesterton, Cambridge. The ferries were placed across the river and connected to each other with wooden planks to form a floating bridge.
Cambridgeshire Collection, Cambridgeshire Libraries

that—"should it be possible to overcome the navigational difficulties at some future date, the vehicular ferry service should then be restored and pending the restoration of the ferry service, a temporary bridge should be erected."

A very ancient ferry existed at **Woodbridge**, Suffolk, linking the town to the village of Sutton on the eastern side of the river. Its actual origin cannot be traced but evidence suggests it operated in feudal times "since the memory of man runneth not to the contrary." It was still functioning as recently as 1974, in spite of the many attempts on the part of the Woodbridge Council to close it and the fact that it was losing money.

This ferry across the River Deben has had a very chequered career. Its modern history began when John Cobbold, a brewer, was tenant of the ferry from 1883 until the end of the First World War.

On 27th June 1919 he conveyed it by Deed of Gift to the Council so that it could be held by the Council for ever for the benefit of the public. Throughout the period between the two world wars the Council let the ferry to various boatmen, giving them the right to run the ferry and collect the fares.

In an article entitled *Transport Topics*, H. E. Wilton quotes a reference to the ferry from Thomas Wright's *Life of Edward Fitzgerald.*

> "You knock at a slatted box, which has a high tiny window and 'F.H.' on the door, and a man in blue, with leggings and woollen socks, appears and takes you over in a boat, which he propels by pushing an oar into the mud. To make known your desire to return he says—'You must holler.'"

This was in 1856.

Later a fourteen foot motor boat was in operation. The ferry provided the easiest and quickest route to and from Woodbridge, the alternative necessitated a journey of about eight miles for schools, shopping, business or pleasure and a long walk as well as a long ride by crowded and infrequent buses.

By August 1949 bus services had improved and the Council claimed that they were running the ferry at a considerable loss each year. They pointed out that they could apply for an Act of Parliament to close or dispose of the ferry, or run a limited service. They decided to experiment by operating with restricted winter working hours and increased fares. However, losses continued.

A year later the Council made known their intention of promoting a Bill in Parliament to close the ferry altogether. However, 70 residents signed a petition that the ferry be maintained and the Council took a poll: this they lost and the possible promotion of the Bill had to be dropped because any method of extinguishing the ferry rights would depend almost entirely on there being no inconvenience caused to the public if the ferry were not operated. It seemed that there was a considerable body of opinion against the closure and a number of people had stated they still used the ferry.

Raising the fares over the years from 2d. (0.83p) return, the original figure, to 10p (2/-) in 1974, did little to help for the Council claimed that each passenger was costing them £2.50. At that time a local boatyard was paid £3 weekly to operate the ferry, but in two years it was used only by 140 people. Temporary repairs had to be made to the landing stage and river bank on the Sutton side, followed by permanent repairs later, which were estimated to cost between £2,000 and £3,000. There was also the cost of replacing the boat.

The history of Woodbridge Ferry during this century alone is an indication of the problems which can be encountered by owners of ferries held under franchise, who are compelled to carry on a service if there is sufficient demand for it, even if it is losing money. But then, as a boat builder and former ferryman argued—"Maybe not many people use it—but if there's an unfrequented street in a town you don't pull it up!"

The **Felixstoweferry to Bawdsey Quay** service was apparently in operation by the twelfth century. Little is recorded about the earliest period of the ferry's history but the service was a foot ferry maintained by rowing boats, passengers' horses having to swim across.

It was not until August 1894 that this ancient ferry was replaced by a steam-chain ferry provided by Sir Cuthbert Quilter of Bawdsey Manor, who constantly used his own boat on the river. This was well patronised but by 1926 it was running at a heavy loss and reverted to rowing and motor boats from about 1930 onwards.

The two chain pontoons which operated on this passage for about forty years were the *Lady Quilter* and the *Lady Beatrice*, the smaller of the two being used in the winter and as a reserve. They were described as "clanking, clattering contrivances with a deck house and smoking chimney complete with warning whistle and a great sight, especially when the cargo was a coach-and-four complete with the top-hatted coachman and sounding horn."

The withdrawal of the vehicular service in 1931 resulted in such traffic having to cross the river by Wilford Bridge at Melton, about ten miles upstream of the ferry site.

During the period 1920/25 the annual traffic was about 12,600 pedestrians, 5,600 cycles and 2,400 vehicles. When the Air Ministry opened their R.A.F. Station at Bawdsey Charlie Brinkley, the ferryman, was paid £250 a month to run the ferry for its men. He was able to employ two part-time helpers then. The 1948 D.o.T. Report referred to the Air Ministry's use of the ferry, estimating that the resulting service traffic desiring crossing facilities at this point included 2,400 passengers a week and this was the only crossing of the Deben within the limits of the Suffolk Coast and Heaths Conservation Area proposed by the National Parks Committee. They therefore recommended that the vehicular service should be restored and its capacity should not be less than when it was last operated and a regular service should be operated at weekdays and Sundays.

In spite of the Ferries Committee Report it has not been found possible to restore the vehicular service, and the present passenger ferry is not paying its way. For two winters after Bawdsey radar station closed in 1975, Mr Brinkley received a £15 a week subsidy from Suffolk Coastal District Council, to keep the ferry running every day.

The *Lady Quilter* chain ferry on the crossing from Felixstoweferry to Bawdsey Quay. *JV-R Collection*

"The trouble was," said Charlie Brinkley, "no more than four people used it. At my age, 72, I no longer want to be tied to the job all hours in all kinds of weather. If anyone else wants to do it, taking £6 a week in fares, they are welcome."

At present he confines the crossing between Bawdsey and Felixstowe to a Saturday morning shuttle to link with the Felixstowe buses, simply to enable a small local community to shop in that town. He resumes the daily service in the summer, which is the only time when he can be sure of breaking even.

Even when the R.A.F. Camp is opened again, in 1980, as a Coastal Defence Base, they are unlikely to need a contract passenger ferry across the Deben estuary. It is reported that they are expected to turn more to Woodbridge.

In his book—*Ferries and Ferrymen*—Bernard Wood writes of Stephen Laud who was a ferryman of some renown. For many years he worked the ferry service across Harwich Harbour from Landguard Fort built to guard the river mouth on the point opposite Harwich, Essex, and seaward of the present port of Felixstowe, Suffolk. Its chief purpose was to carry parcels and letters for the Fort and to convey soldiers to and from Harwich, but it also transported civilians on their way to London.

The present ferry serving **Felixstowe and Harwich** is a passenger ferry operated by the Orwell and Harwich Navigation Company Ltd., under the management of Mrs Gwendoline Goodhew. When I crossed the ferry from Felixstowe Dock to meet her in her office at Harwich Pier, she told me that, in 1912, the Great Eastern Railway—now British Rail— acquired the ferry rights and operated a regular service for the benefit of railway passengers and holiday makers. The nearest alternative route between Harwich and Felixstowe was via Manningtree and Ipswich, a distance of about 36 miles.

Mrs Goodhew said her husband had purchased the ferry rights from British Rail in 1962. She described him as having been prepared to work long hours for small financial returns on a job in which he was interested. When he died, in 1970, she had to decide whether or not to take over the ferry, about which she had no practical experience. British Rail had sold the business because they could not make it pay, and as her husband had invested their capital in the ferry, and worked hard for small financial reward, she decided to keep the ferry. Having been a housewife with three sons to educate, she took over a ship.

Now the motor vessel *Brightlingsea* operates every day from the end of April until the beginning of October. It operates from each side at hourly intervals, with an hour's break at midday, taking 20 minutes on the crossing and 10 minutes wait between crossings. The service is run by covered launch in winter and two scheduled services run from Mondays to Fridays, one in the morning and another in the evening timed to suit business people wishing to cross. There is no Saturday, Sunday or Bank Holiday service in the winter. Fares in 1978 were 45p and 25p for children. The ferry is timed to connect with bus services from Felixstowe Dock into Felixstowe and on to Ipswich. A 24-hour service is maintained 7 days a week on demand for those wishing to cross the Harbour.

Those going to work use the ferry in early morning and for the return in the evening and ships' papers and parcels are taken over. These can be delivered in fifteen minutes from the time of arrival at the ferry.

A coxswain and mate operate the *Brightlingsea*, a diesel vessel 71 feet overall, 16 feet beam, with a speed of 8-12 knots. It was one of the first diesel ferries and is licensed to carry 174 passengers. There is considerable tourist traffic in the summer and quite a number of cyclists cross with their bicycles. It carries the requisite number of life buoys, life rafts, smoke flares and an Aldis lamp, and is equipped with radar, depth sounder and V.H.F. Radio.

Feasibility studies have shown that a change to a car ferry would be financially uneconomic, and the ferry continues to be a passenger ferry.

In order to make it pay Mrs Goodhew has found it necessary to use the ferry boat for cruises on summer evenings and, with a bar and buffet, these are extremely popular, enabling passengers to enjoy the beauty of the rivers Orwell and Stour.

Lindsey's *Season At Harwich 1851* refers to the wherry which "should be waiting at Walton Ferry to convey a party across the bay to Harwich and from there the ladies should be rowed from the Naval Yard to Shotley Ferry and travel to Ipswich from there by the steam boat *River Queen* that plies on the Orwell."

Shotley to Harwich Ferry, known later as Bristol's Ferry, appears in the Doomsday Book of 1085. In 1286 proceedings were taken against Guy Visdelou, holding the tenure of Shotley Manor, who answered to the King, Edward I, about his claim to have wreck of the sea and other franchises in connection with his manor at Shotley. Guy Visdelou said that he and his ancestors had held these franchises from time immemorial.

In 1886, six hundred years later, Lord Bristol, lineal descendant of Guy Visdelou, was also involved in proceedings with the Court for the same reason. His defence was that his predecessors had always treated the foreshore as theirs and had made sea walls on the foreshore and reclaimed land which had been part of the foreshore. He also added that the ancient ferry had belonged to his family as did the landing place and quay on the foreshore which were maintained by them.

Hervey claims, in the Shotley Parish Records, that the ferry boat had been rowed between Shotley and Harwich from exactly the same point to exactly the same point from time immemorial and that the *Bristol Arms* may stand on the site of the ferryman's house, which was in such a position that it would catch everybody going to the ferry whether they came from Manningtree or Ipswich.

Yet it would appear, from the following extract of an address to the electors of Harwich and Dovercourt on 24th December, 1834, by R. N. Verner, Captain of the 61st Regiment, that there was no ferry at Shotley at that time:-

"Long before I ever calculated on offering myself to represent you in Parliament, I was employed in arranging plans to improve your Town, Harbour, and reclaim from the sea such of the land as would be practicable, together with connecting you, in the direction of Shotley, by means of a Floating Bridge for Foot-Passengers, Carriages and Waggons. The Plan is in my possession; I brought it from India; it will be perfectly safe and will be so constructed as not to impede either Passengers or Vessels at any state of the Tide. This being once established you can build public baths, improve your Beach and erect Marine Villas.

I also propose to make this a Depot for Fish and Oysters, to enable the Hungerford Market Small Steamers (of which I am a Proprietor), to call here, to take Passengers and Fish to London.

In addition to all these improvements, there should be a Public Garden. as thousands of visitors would be induced to spend their money with you. My only reason for wishing to represent you in Parliament is that I should then be enabled, by having greater influence, to carry my Plans into effect.

The expense of the Bridge will not be heavy and it will pay for itself by the Tolls. I have several Relations and Friends, who have empowered me to employ their Capital in any safe enterprise; and I shall be happy to enrol the names of any Persons who feel inclined to form a Company, in Shares not less than Five Pounds, or exceeding £500. I will place myself at the Head of the List. As a Shareholder for Five Hundred Pounds.

I beg to offer my unqualified opinion that there is no other permanent mode in which I can plan that will make Harwich a wealthy and happy town. I offer my services to you without any remuneration beyond your good opinion of my zeal and sincerity to make this Shamefully-Neglected, but beautiful Spot, superior to any Watering-Place in the Kingdom . . . "

Mrs Winifred Cooper, Chairman of the Harwich Society, sent me a copy of this address adding—"He did not get in, as Harwich was one of the 'rotten' boroughs in the pocket of the Government, and we did not get our Floating Bridge, and all the other goodies!"

It would appear from the foregoing that the ferry had ceased to operate for a period around 1834.

It had long ceased to operate when a friend drove me to Shotley on a fine Sunday morning at the end of September 1977, but we found some retired ferrymen at the Yacht Club who told us that it used to run every hour from Bristol Pier to Harwich Pier and Felixstowe, with 10 minutes for each stop. The alternative was a 20-mile journey by road.

There are, or were, other ferries in Suffolk; one for instance, shown in an **Ipswich** handbook of 1864 says—"Ferry boats cross the river at two or three points" and in the Court of Common Council (1600-1644) it was ordered that George Hudson, or Hodson, should pay 1d weekly in "consideration of his ferry to Ipswich each Saturday being market day" and a scale of charges for the ferry was drawn up, the single fare being fixed at 1d. In 1613 Hudson's rent of the ferry was 10s. 0d. per annum. Doubtless this ferry was running long before this item was minuted.

Engraving of Shotley Ferry, 1830 *Mrs Winifred Cooper*

CHAPTER THREE

London River

IN HIS book, *Crossing London's River,* John Pudney writes: "There is the river from Thames Head to the Nore, only just over double the length of the Suez Canal, yet so burdened and fringed with history that it defies the compass of any single book. The tidal reaches, 69 miles in length, serve Greater London, and this tideway is crossed by a somewhat haphazard pattern of bridges, tunnels and ferries . . . "

Ferries proliferated across the Thames before bridges were built but today it is the bridges and tunnels which, with very few exceptions, take traffic over and under the Thames.

Twickenham Ferry is scarcely remembered except by local historians who may recall that the ferryman, Walter Hammerton, stood out for his ferrying rights, even appealing successfully to the House of Lords when all else failed, following which he was made a Freeman of the City of London. As recently as Edwardian and late Victorian times 2,000 people crossed this ferry on Bank Holidays.

Coming nearer inner London, **Chelsea Ferry** is but a memory, although it was of ancient origin and was certainly in existence in the time of James I. It ceased to operate when Putney Bridge was built in 1750, but the petition by the Chelsea ferryman for compensation on account of consequent loss of business was not upheld because of the distance between the ferry and the new bridge.

When Lambeth Bridge was erected, in 1729, the see of Canterbury was awarded compensation for the loss of ferry rights there.

Horseferry Road is still a reminder of that ancient horse ferry at **Lambeth** which, from time immemorial, plied across the river where Lambeth Bridge joins bank to bank.

This ferry had a bad reputation according to Nicholas Hawksmore who wrote in his *Short Historical Account of London Bridge* "There is no need to say anything of the badness and inconvenience of Lambeth Ferry since there is scarce anyone ignorant of it and some have found it to their cost."

Doubtless his comments were made partly because of several accidents which occurred. In 1633, for example, Archbishop Laud's arrival at Lambeth was marked by an accident on the over-laden ferry boat as it crossed with his servants and horsemen. It sank to the bottom of the Thames, though without loss of human life.

Two old ferryboats, the *Gordon* (left) and the *Squires* operated on the Woolwich Free Ferry opened by Lord Rosebery, Chairman of the London County Council, on 23rd March 1889.
Greater London Council

Again, in 1656, when the Proctor's coach and horses were crossing in the ferry at Lambeth the boat sank. This time the coach sank and three horses were drowned.

During the Civil War in 1648, the ferry was confiscated with the rest of the Archbishop's property. The rights reverted to the Archbishop on Restoration but his successors did not carry out their obligation, for complaints were made by Church wardens and inhabitants of the Parish of St Margaret's that they "usurped the whole profits of the horse ferry and neglected to repair the roads leading thereto."

It is interesting to note the fees charged on this ferry in 1708.

For a man and horse	2d.
For a horse and chase	1s. 0d.
For a coach and 2 horses	1s. 6d.
For a coach and 4	2s. 0d.
For a coach and 6	2s. 6d.
For a cart laden	2s. 6d.
For a cart or waggon	2s. 0d.

The old ferry house existed for a hundred years after the ferry ceased to operate. It is referred to by Dickens, who was familiar with so many of London's ferries. In *David Copperfield* he writes:-

> "There was, and is as I write, at the end of that low-lying street, a dilapidated little wooden building probably an old ferry house."

There were many other ferries, such as those at Deptford, Greenwich and the Isle of Dogs, but the two which have survived and are the best known are those at **Woolwich** and **Gravesend/Tilbury**.

The people of Woolwich have had a right to run a ferry from the time when it was a small fishing village. The ferry ran between North Woolwich and Warren Lane on the south shore.

There is an early reference to this ferry in the State papers of 1308 when the ferry changed hands, a proceeding which occurred on two other occasions, first in 1320 and again in 1340, when "several acres of land, rent in Woolwich, and the ferry" were conveyed to Thomas Harold and his heirs, for 100 silver marks.

In 1330 the people of Woolwich petitioned Parliament to suppress rival ferries at Greenwich and Erith because that at Woolwich was a "Royal Ferry", favoured of the King, which probably means it was an appurtenance of the royal manor of Eltham until Henry VIII's time.

As London grew bigger and busier the Royal Arsenal, which was established at Woolwich as an ordnance depot in Henry VIII's reign, was faced with the problem of coping with the movement of troops and supplies into Essex. Therefore, in 1810 the Army established its own ferry which went from the "T" pier in front of the Arsenal to Duval's Point, the Old Barge House landing site, on the northern bank.

In 1811 another ferry was established by Act of Parliament operating from the **Old Ballast**, or Sand Wharf, to where the dockyard then terminated. This was to be a "common ferry, consisting of one or more boats, or such other vessel as shall be sufficient and proper for the passage and conveyance of persons, carriages, cattle, goods, wares and merchandise over the said River Thames . . . " The Woolwich Ferry Company was formed, the shareholders including the Lady of the Manor and her son, but the Minute books of the Waterman's Company show that the watermen of Woolwich were very dissatisfied with the monopoly given to the "western ferry" by the 1811 Act, wherein a penalty of 40s. (increased to £5 in the 1815 Amendment) was imposed on anyone carrying any person, carriage or chattel over the water within half a mile of it. This was increased to 2 miles in the 1815 Amendment.

Its promoters asserted that as it was half a mile from the town it did not prejudice the inhabitants of Woolwich or the watermen. In 1816 the watermen petitioned for a repeal of the Act, and were successful.

However, the western ferry continued to run until 1844 when the company was dissolved. Not only had the thousands of pounds raised by shares and mortgages been swallowed up in unprofitable expenditure, but there was no mention in the accounts of revenue derived from the working of the ferry, neither had any dividend been distributed to the unfortunate shareholders. In fact, the ferry had a history of inept management and general confusion.

With the decline of its rival's fortunes the **Barge House Ferry** at the Warren Lane Crossing improved. In 1839 it was reported—"The lessees of Woolwich ferry have, within the last few weeks, stationed here a new ferry boat of larger dimensions than any on the river with a view to meeting the increase of traffic that has lately taken place between the two counties. Mr Hose, the proprietor of The Old Barge House is constructing an esplanade extending along the banks of the river 300 yards, the depth upwards of 130 feet."

The greater part of this esplanade was later incorporated in the Royal Victoria Gardens.

In 1846 the Great Eastern Railway Company extended its line along the river bank to the old horse ferry which crossed the river to Woolwich and ran three ferry boats, the *Kent, Essex* and *Middlesex*, to connect with London trains.

The ferry changed hands several times in the next few years, and from 1850 onwards there were proposals for superseding the ancient horse raft of Woolwich Ferry by a steam vessel, the idea being a flat-bottomed boat grounding on the beach, but nothing was actually done about this until 1880 by which time the existing means of crossing the river were rapidly becoming inadequate. A public meeting was held to see whether the parish could afford to set up its own steam ferry. A deputation of sixty townsfolk waited on the Local Board but it was decided that the cost of building the boats and landing piers was too great and representations were made to the Metropolitan Board of Works, forerunners of the London County Council. The people of Woolwich pointed out that through their rates they had helped to pay for the toll bridges in West London which the Board had recently bought and opened to free public use, and suggested that they too should be able to cross the Thames free of charge.

The people of Woolwich must have been delighted with the success of their representations. In 1884, after making a general survey of existing communications across the Thames, the Metropolitan Board of Works agreed to provide the ferry and, in the Metropolitan Board of Works (Various Powers) Act of 1885, obtained statutory authority to ferry across the Thames at Woolwich, passengers, animals, vehicles and goods, free of all tolls, rates and charges.

Sites were acquired and in September 1887 Mowlem and Company were given the contract to make the approaches, bridge and pontoons. On 23rd March 1889 the Free Ferry was opened by Lord Rosebery, Chairman of the London County Council, the Metropolitan Board of Works having ceased to exist three days previously.

It is not surprising to read that the ceremony took place amidst quite extraordinary rejoicing. Woolwich was arrayed in flags and bunting. The streets were lined with volunteers of the 2nd Kent (Plumstead) Artillery, the 3rd Kent (Royal Arsenal) Artillery, and the 3rd Kent (Royal Arsenal) Rifles. Preceded by mounted police, marched a procession of the various local trade and friendly societies with their emblems and bands and the boys of the Marine Society from the *Warspite*, also with a band. Behind came the official party driving in open carriages. Lord Rosebery and other members of the London County Council were there, the local Member of Parliament for Woolwich, and other district representatives.

The procession headed for the river where the *Gordon*, 490 tons gross, 164 feet in length, with an extreme breadth over the sponsons of 60 feet, was waiting to take the whole procession across to North Woolwich where they were met by another procession which included the decorated steam fire engine of Beckton Gas Works. Half an hour later the party recrossed the Thames when Lord Rosebery, standing in the carriage before a stand of 600 people, declared the ferry open, free for ever.

The day concluded with a banquet for 200 guests at the Freemasons' Hall.

Altogether it was a marvellous send-off for a ferry of which the citizens of Woolwich are justly proud, and which has become known far and wide as Woolwich Free Ferry.

The diesel-engined ferry boat, *John Burns*, was built at Dundee in 1963. The vessel is shown here on the maintenance grid at Woolwich which is adjacent to the marine workshop.
Greater London Council

The total cost of the scheme was £191,444. The three boats, one of which, the *Hutton*, was built later, cost £45,077, the works of construction cost £75,907 and the acquisition of the necessary land, with the amounts paid in compensation, £67,081. This last figure included compensation for loss of income to the Watermen and Lightermen of Woolwich, to the Woolwich (Old Barge House) Steam Ferry Company, which went into liquidation, and £27,500 to the Great Eastern Railway Company which continued to run its own ferry until 1908.

All this took place just ninety years ago. Much has happened since that time.

Soon after their construction the three paddle steamers, the *Gordon, Duncan,* and *Hutton*, were fitted with electric light throughout, a fact reported with pride at the time. They were driven by two pairs of engines, each pair being connected to one paddle-wheel. They were capable of eight knots and licensed to carry 1,000 passengers with room for fifteen to twenty vehicles. The lower deck was for passengers, the upper for vehicles. Access to the traffic deck was from the upper deck of the pontoon by lowering prows worked by hydraulic machinery. In time these first three boats were replaced by four similar new ones, also paddle steamers. These were the *Squires,* the *Gordon,* the *John Benn* and *Will Crooks.* Because of the limited depth of water at the pontoons at low tide the loaded draught of the boats had to be kept at about five feet.

There was no doubting the pleasure derived by the many people using this free ferry. Mothers took their children and a picnic basket for an afternoon on board the old boats to watch the ships passing, the local children enjoyed countless free rides to and fro across the Thames in their spare time; radio shows were broadcast from the boats and they were photographed by numerous boating enthusiasts. By the time the old paddle steamers finished their service they had travelled some 400,000 miles in journeys across the Thames, carried 180 million passengers and 55 million vehicles and cycles. They plied in all kinds of weathers and in all but the thickest fog, although once a ferry boat missed her mooring in the fog and drifted up Woolwich Reach, crew and passengers being forced to spend the night aboard.

Since its inauguration the ferry has only been closed three times; once in the General Strike of 1926, when labour was withdrawn for a fortnight and there was a disciplinary enquiry, again in 1926 after a collision with an American ship, and for three months in 1949 when the pontoons were removed for docking and repair.

The ferries had their hour of glory during the war, although they did not go to Dunkirk. On the night of the big docks raid of 7th September 1940 they plied to and fro all night evacuating the people of Silvertown from the blazing Essex shore and taking them, together with all their goods and chattels, from

The *James Newman*, like the *John Burns*, was built for the Woolwich Free Ferry at Dundee in 1963. The vessel is here seen in service loaded with vehicles and passengers.
Greater London Council

furniture to canaries, over to Kent across a River Thames scattered with burning oil. All through the war the ferry was running a 24-hour service as and when it was needed and, for a while, in the blackout they were allowed no guiding light whatever. Steering was even more difficult by the fact that the bridge was closed in with concrete slabs as a protection against shrapnel. On one occasion a bomb exploded just beneath the stern of one of the boats but did not do enough damage to put the boat out of service. Another time a V.1 just missed the bridge of the boat and buried itself in the far bank of the river.

The quick thinking of the mate avoided what might have been a tragic incident in 1926. The *Squires* arrived alongside the south pontoon at 5.42 p.m. on 29th June, with 400 passengers on board. The rope had just been made fast when the mate who was in charge of the ship noticed a large steamer steering a peculiar course and heading down river towards the ferry boat. He gave orders to let go the ropes and went astern full speed with his engines, though he could not avoid a collision completely. The ship, *Coahoma County*, 5,590 tons gross, owned by the U.S. Shipping Board, struck the ferry a crushing blow on the port bow forward and caused it to rebound on to the pontoon, doing considerable damage. No one was injured but had the steamer hit the *Squires* as she was moored, she would probably have sunk with considerable loss of life.

As a result the ferry service could not be resumed until 9th August.

The ferries were often subject to hold-ups due to fog and Thames shipping and people were delayed sometimes on their way to work. When the

Railway Ferry service withdrew in 1908 the free ferry boats became more crowded and the Council sought powers to build a foot tunnel, which had long been under discussion. Four years later the foot tunnel was opened.

The paddle steamers were designed for side-loading, which was satisfactory for horse-drawn vehicles and the smaller volume of vehicular traffic of the past, but with larger heavier and articulated type of motor vehicles, loading by this means was a long and complicated process. These vehicles were difficult to stow and there were longer delays at the terminals yet the number of vehicles on the roads was increasing. It was, therefore, decided to replace the existing vessels with modern end-loading diesel vessels and to build a causeway on each side of the river, terminating at mechanically-operated hinged traffic bridges to make loading and off-loading easier. Improvements to the approaches to the ferry were also decided upon.

Three diesel-engined ferry boats were constructed in 1963 by the Caleden Shipbuilding and Engineering Co. Ltd., Dundee, at a total contract price of £804,000. Each was licensed to carry 500 passengers and 200 tons of vehicles. They were designed so that they could be used as side-loaders at the old terminals while the new terminals were being built, but were readily convertible to end-loading when the new adjacent terminals were completed. End-loading permits vehicles to drive on at one end and off at the other without complicated manoeuvres and with the least possible delay. The ferries are double-ended, able to proceed equally in either direction, and able to leave the terminals in a down-stream direction whatever the state of the tide. They are propelled by two pressure charged Mirless National 500 h.p. diesel engines which drive two Voith-Schneider Cycloidal Propellers, one fitted each end of the boat. This provides the high degree of manoeuvrability essential in the tidal waters at Woolwich. The propellers are controlled from any one of three consoles placed in the centre and at each end of the navigational bridge, which is situated amidships. The boats are named the *John Burns,* the *Ernest Bevin,* and the *James Newman* after three pioneering politicians, all connected in some way with Woolwich or the Thames.

These boats provide the link between the North and South Circular Roads and it is expected that they will be able to cope with the increasingly heavy traffic. In the twelve months ending 1st April 1973 a total of 6,190,601 cars and 323,106 lorries were ferried in both directions, the boats making 48,329 trips.

The Free Ferry has a statutory obligation to run at certain times every day of the year and this is probably the busiest of all the river ferries. The time taken on embarkation and disembarkation is approximately fifteen minutes, while the journey across the ferry takes five minutes.

There are seven crew members and one shipkeeper who cleans the vessel and watchmen are on duty when the vessel is not in service. Just over 900 journeys are made each week, this with an incentive scheme, the busiest period being commuter times, from 7 until 9 in the morning, and again from 4.30 to 6 o'clock in the evening.

Berthing requires a terrific amount of practice, I was told. There is a lot of weight and power behind the ferry and an error on the part of the master, just jarring the jetty, could mean a slight shifting of vehicles.

Every year 350 to 400 handicapped children are taken for a trip on the river on a summer afternoon, when Tower Bridge is specially raised for their benefit. The ferry's Social Committee arranged to meet the cost of £400 by sponsored walks, social events and contributions from local business people.

It is obvious that Woolwich Free Ferry has justified and still is justifying its existence with a continously running service all through the year.

Another well known ferry is that from **Gravesend to Tilbury**. Originally there were two passages known as the Long Ferry and the Cross Ferry. The Long Ferry was probably in use before the Norman Conquest, conveying passengers and goods from the Kent or the Essex side of the river to and from London. Travellers coming from the Continent and landing at Dover took the Dover Road to Gravesend and then the Long Ferry to London, this being the best and quickest route at that time. Not only did the roads on either side of the river provide no direct route to London, but they were in a very bad condition.

But it is the Short Ferry, or Cross Ferry, which is still operating across the Thames. Its date of origin is not clear, but it is one of the oldest in the south-eastern region. As far as is known no trace has been found of any granting of a Royal Charter, but it is thought that a form of rights was

The steam ferry *Tilbury* with passengers on the Tilbury to Gravesend crossing. The *Tilbury* was the first paddle steamer on this service. *A. Jarvis*

exercised for many years by the Lords of the Manors of Tilbury and Parrock and by virtue of the continual exercising of these rights in connection with the ferry a monopoly developed and this monopoly became a privilege and then an acknowledged right. There are many instances of such series of events relating to similar concessions during medieval times. At any rate, the Lords of Tilbury and Parrock were responsible for the ferry until 1540, when Tilbury Fort was built, at which time the ferry became associated with it, the public right of way actually passing through the Fort, which posed problems during the Civil War. Until that time the ferry crossed the river between East Tilbury and Tower Higham but, with the growth of Gravesend in the reign of Henry VII, it was moved up river to the Three Crowns landing stage, which since the early nineteenth century has been known as the Ferry House.

The story of Charles I crossing this ferry in disguise in 1623, when he was Prince of Wales, has been told frequently. Accompanied by the Duke of Buckingham he was on his way to woo the Infanta of Spain. The Duke gave the ferryman a gold piece to cover the fare, whereupon, thinking they were spies or that they were travelling to fight an illegal duel, the ferryman had them arrested.

In 1694-5 Gravesend Corporation acquired the Manor of Parrock and purchased the ferry rights. An arrangement was then made between the Corporation and the officer commanding Tilbury Fort giving him the right to the Essex end of the ferry; also the right to build a public house there. This he eventually did, building it for the convenience of the passengers and as a dwelling house for his ferrymen. This is the well-known *World's End* public house and the causeway on the Tilbury side of the ferry is known by that name. It has another interest for it features in the marshland scenes in Charles Dickens' *Great Expectations.*

The Tilbury side of the ferry was now in the hands of the Board of Ordnance. In 1799, during the national crisis precipitated by the War of American Independence, 5,000 troops with Ordnance were, in the course of training, conveyed in barges warped over by hawsers extended across the river. The double crossing was completed between 6 a.m. and 4 p.m. Fourteen years later hawsers were abandoned and troops were ferried over in barges towed by sailing vessels or, in calm water, by rowing boats.

In the year 1850 the Board of Ordnance were making demands upon the Corporation of Gravesend for an improved ferry service. The Corporation argued that such a service would only be possible if the rights of the ferry in both directions were in the same hands and eventually, in September 1851, the Corporation of Gravesend took over the lease from the Board of Ordnance of the Tilbury to Gravesend Ferry at a rental of £50 per annum on a ninety-nine year lease. For the first time in its history, as far as is known, the ferry rights in both directions were in the hands of one party.

In September 1851 the Corporation leased the rights in both directions to William Tisdoll of Gravesend, but despite promises made by the Corporation to the Board of Ordnance the ferry service did not improve to the satisfaction of the Officer Commanding Tilbury Fort. In November 1854 the Board of Ordnance threatened that unless proper ferry services were available forthwith they would have to consider terminating the lease between the Corporation and themselves. The Corporation therefore terminated the lease to Tisdoll and the ferry rights passed into the hands of Peto, Betts and Brassey on behalf of the London, Tilbury and Southend Railway Company as from 18th February 1856 for a term of twenty-four years at a rental of £750 a year.

The Gravesend terminus had a long causeway, satisfactory when the ferry was maintained by wherries, but not so with the advent of steamers in 1834. The town pier was therefore adapted and the first of the steam ferries, the *Tilbury*, came into service, to be followed by the *Carlotta*. In the early years of the twentieth century the *Rose, Catherine, Gertrude* and *Edith* were built, remaining in service until 1961, except the *Gertrude* which was withdrawn in 1930.

The Town Pier belonged to the Corporation and the Railway Company was forced to give part of each fare taken to that body, 1d. out of the 4d. fare. Arguments were frequent and the Railway Company then built their own pier in West Street and only charged a 3d. fare. Eventually the West Street Pier was used for cattle traffic and the Town Pier for passengers, cattle being discharged at the World's End Causeway, and passengers at the landing stage at Tilbury.

When the Midland Railway bought the London, Tilbury and Southend Railway it also acquired the ferry but made few alterations. In 1914 workmen's season tickets were introduced, 1s. 3d. a week, the daily return fare being 3d., and a workman's ticket 2d.

The Department of Trade reported on the position of this ferry in 1948 as follows:-

> "The equipment of the vehicular ferry consists of two beam loading vessels, of which one is in operation and the other in reserve, plying between floating landing stages connected with the land by bridges. One of these vessels can carry 30 cars and 4 lorries. The capacity of the other is 25 cars and 3 lorries. When loaded to capacity the first vehicle on is normally the last off. There is a half-hourly service for the greater part of the day on weekdays and Sundays, but the service is sometimes interrupted by fog. The Royal Commission on Cross River Traffic in London reported, in 1926, that this ferry appeared to be used then to full capacity. The ferry serves both industrial needs and long distance tourist traffic. It appears that, in the summer months, the ferry is sometimes unable to

accommodate all the waiting vehicles. The approaches to the ferry at Gravesend are narrow and may deter some types of traffic. The ultimate completion of the Dartford Purfleet Tunnel and the associated new roads will have the effect of reducing the traffic demand for this crossing."

The Committee completed its report by adding that while improvements were desirable, they would make no recommendation in view of the fact that work had commenced on construction of the tunnel, which had for long been under discussion.

The number of vehicles using the ferry gradually increased between the years 1954-1958 when they totalled 280,000.

In February 1959, the British Transport Commission announced that, having considered the future impact on the ferry service of the Dartford-Purfleet Tunnel, which was due to be opened in 1962, they considered that the demand then for vehicular ferries would be too small to justify the building of costly replacements of vessels, but the demand for passenger service would continue. However, the railways had now come under the control of British Railways and in September the Eastern Region decided to seek Parliamentary permission to end their legal obligation to produce a vehicle ferry. At the same time they decided to replace their steam passenger ferries with diesel vessels, 110 feet in length, to take 400 passengers. These were replaced in January 1962 and British Railways finally withdrew their vehicle ferry on 31st December 1964.

Following the closure of the vehicle ferry, passenger traffic on the river began to show a decline until, in 1973, and again in 1977, there was talk of British Rail having to close the ferry as it was losing several thousands of pounds a year. No one wanted to see the ferry close, not the million or so passengers using it each year, nor British Rail, least of all the ferrymen, many of whom had been on the river all their lives.

When I crossed on the ferry one mid-morning in July 1977, though doubtless passenger traffic was plentiful in commuter time, things were so quiet that it was not surprising that British Rail had their doubts about the advisability of continuing operating the ferry. Yet tradition dies hard and for commuters the ferry was still worthwhile, and for Albert Jarvis, the mate on duty now nearing retirement who told me he had spent his life working on the river, following the example of his father who had been connected with the ferry for forty-seven years. Starting as a boy of fourteen Albert Jarvis first worked on the Gravesend tugs and after three years joined the Gravesend/Tilbury Ferry service as a deck boy. That was in 1909, when he earned 5s. 0d. a week. By the time he retired he had been senior ferry captain for ten years.

He started on the paddle-steamer *Thames* when only one boat was running and most of the traffic was horse-drawn. Then there were only about twelve cars a day to be ferried across the river but before he retired they sometimes had as many as twelve hundred.

During the course of his years on the ferry he had helped to rescue a number of people. Perhaps the most spectacular was the rescue of a woman who had slipped overboard when endeavouring to leave the ferry at the Town Pier. The accident could have had fatal consequences, for the woman passed completely under the steamer and, although Albert Jarvis immediately dived in, fully clothed, she had come up for the second time before he effected her rescue. For this act of bravery, performed at the risk of his own life, he was awarded the Royal Humane Society's Certificate.

The Tilbury to Gravesend Ferry *Mimie*. *A. Jarvis*

The Sealink Ferry, *Cenred,* on the Lymington to Yarmouth, Isle of Wight, crossing.

Sealink UK Limited

CHAPTER FOUR

Mainland to the Isle of Wight

THE Isle of Wight, which lies four miles across the Solent from the South Coast towns of Portsmouth, Southampton and Lymington, is the easiest of access of any of the islands off the coast of England. Referring to the mainland as England has become a hackneyed joke, yet once the call—"Any more for England!"—was heard nightly at the end of Yarmouth pier when passengers left on the last ferry for Lymington.

Today all Isle of Wight ferries from **Portsmouth**, also those from **Lymington to Yarmouth**, are operated by Sealink UK Ltd .but Bernard Wood, in his book *Ferries and Ferrymen*, records that, in 1420 "the Abbess Wherwell controlled the boats which took passengers over the Solent to Portsmouth," and in 1604 the annual Court Leet enacted that there should be no Sunday ferry service unless a fare could prove he was on the king's business or carried a special warrant from the Lord of the Manor.

Lymington has an even earlier history, for it was reputedly known to and used by the Phoenicians, and later occupied by the Romans. By the fourteenth century Lymington was larger than Portsmouth and contributed nearly twice as many ships and men to Edward II's fleet for the invasion of France. It also has historical associations with Charles I, the Civil War and Monmouth's rebellion in 1685.

The castle to be seen on the port side of the ferry when coming into Yarmouth was built by order of Henry VIII, while the last seamark on coming out of Lymington is Jack in the Basket. This was said to be one of the oldest in the British Isles, although it is difficult to verify the truth of this. The story goes that fishermen's wives rowed down the river to drop their husband's dinner in the basket and the men collected them as they sailed past. In the absence of power-assisted craft it would have taken the men too long to get up to town, especially with an off shore wind.

The earliest recorded vessels linking Lymington and Yarmouth were hoys, fore and aft rigged craft from which the expression "ship ahoy" is said to have originated. A tavern in Lymington, which went out of existence many years ago, was known as *The Isle of Wight Hoy*.

I have a photostat copy of an Act of Parliament passed in 1765 in the reign of King George III entitled "An Act for settling the Rates for the Carriage of Passengers and Goods, for Hire, to and from the ISLE OF WIGHT."

This enacts that the Justices of the Peace of the County of Southampton shall rate and assess the "Prices to be taken, as well for the Passage of all Persons as for the Carriage of Cattle, Goods and Merchandise, going to and to be carried from the several places of Passage, in the said Isle of Wight to and from Southampton, Lymington, Portsmouth, Gosport and other places on the Coast of the said County of Southampton, by the several Owners and Masters of all Hoys, Packet Boats and other Vessels whatsoever, kept within the said Island, and usually employed in carrying Passengers, Cattle, Goods or Merchandise, to and from the said Island for Hire . . . "

The document goes on to state that, should "any such Master or Owner, or other Person employed by him demand or take for the Passage of any Person or for the Carriage of any Horses, Cattle or Goods above the rates or prices so to be assessed and rated, or shall refuse or neglect to carry such Passengers, Horses, Cattle or Goods, he shall forfeit the sum of Five Pounds to be levied by distress, or, for want thereof, be committed to the common Goal or House of Correction."

Punishments for neglect of duty were harsh in those days.

Animals had to be driven through the streets of Yarmouth when being dispatched by ferry and a pig was once found in a resident's kitchen. When cars were first carried there was often a delay while the ferry was washed down after a flock of sheep had disembarked.

The first steamer based at Lymington was the *Glasgow*, a wooden-hulled, 17-ton vessel, which commenced service on 5th April 1830. For three days each week she sailed to Portsmouth and back, calling at Yarmouth, Cowes and Ryde. She remained in service from Lymington until 1852. A primitive boat, she was only 52 feet in length and 13 feet breadth. Other and larger vessels followed, especially after the London and South Western Railway Company took over the operation of the Lymington-Yarmouth route to the Island in 1884 when the Lymington Railway was extended from the town to the pier. One of the two ferries the L.S.W.R. purchased from the Solent Steam Packet Company, the previous operators, was the *Solent*. This vessel is notable because in 1897 it was used by Marconi, the pioneer of wireless communication, during his first experiment that year in sending signals over the water, the ferry lying off-shore by the Needles with the shore station at *Needles Hotel* at Alum Bay.

Alfred, Lord Tennyson, crossed from Lymington to Yarmouth on one of the small paddle steamers when on a visit to his old home at Farringford. While crossing, in 1899, he wrote one of his greatest poems—*Crossing the Bar*.

Cars arriving at Fishbourne, Isle of Wight, after being transported from Portsmouth by Tow Boats Two and Three with their tug, *Adur,* in attendance during 1926. *R. Butcher*

The first dual purpose vessel built for this service was the *Lymington* built in 1938 on the Clyde by Denny Brothers of Dumbarton, who have built a number of ships for British Rail Ferries. She was rudderless, her propulsion being by two Voith-Schneider propellers, one each at bow and stern, set diagonally and bridge-controlled. She had a carrying capacity of 516 passengers (390 in winter) or 292 passengers and 16 cars. She was joined by the *Farringford*, a much larger dual-purpose vessel of 489 gross tonnage, diesel-electric-paddle-driven, with a speed of 10½ knots and a carrying capacity of 796 passengers in the summer, or 212 passengers and 36 cars. With the arrival of two still larger ferries in 1973/4, the *Cenred* and *Cenwulf,* the *Farringford* was transferred to Sealink's Humber Services.

The reason for the acquisition of these larger ferries was the increasing car and commercial traffic. The terminal facilities therefore had to be modernised by a new car-ferry loading ramp supported on floating pontoons and new entrance and exit roads at Lymington. Gallery decks were installed later on these new vessels to increase their vehicle-carrying capacity. These vehicles are in use today and can carry 756 passengers, making the crossing in half an hour, their waiting time being forty-five minutes at Yarmouth and fifteen minutes at Lymington. These ships belong to Sealink U.K. Limited, which is a subsidiary of British Railways Board. The normal number of cars carried in summer is 72 with gallery deck in use, and with 756 passengers on

The ferry *Fishbourne* discharging at Fishbourne, Isle of Wight, in January 1963 after a cold passage from Portsmouth. *R. Butcher*

each of these two vessels, but in the past few years commercial traffic has been increasing more than the cars.

In the nineteenth century animals and wheeled vehicles were conveyed in tow boats on the Solent, with a passenger steamer as a tug. The barges were 40/45 feet in length and had a loaded draught of only two feet. Steam tugs were brought into use in 1880. Race horses, on their way to the Island's race meetings held at Ashey Downs, must have endured a most uncomfortable journey.

The service from **Portsmouth to Ryde Sands** was tidal and the tow boat service was discontinued on 13th March 1926 in favour of a new service from Broad Street slipway at **Portsmouth to Fishbourne,** three and a half miles westward of Ryde, where a new slipway had been built. A specially constructed vessel, *Fishbourne,* with hinged prows at each end, lowered to enable vehicles to drive on and off under their own power, entered the service in 1927. She had a speed of 8½ knots and was fitted with four propellers and four rudders, two each at the forward and after ends of the vessel.

It was the intention of the designers that she should operate on the shuttle principle and embark and disembark traffic without the need to swing at the terminals. Under service conditions, however, this was found to be impracticable and eventually she was operated in the same way as one with conventional bow, the two forward rudders being removed and the two forward propellers being used for astern movement only. Vehicles were embarked and disembarked over the stern at Portsmouth and over the bow at Fishbourne, the vessel swinging before arrival at Portsmouth and after departure at Fishbourne. The swinging basin at Fishbourne needed regular dredging owing to constant silting.

Fishbourne's prows were manually operated, a slow and laborious business for four men, but electric winches were fitted later. There were many teething troubles and the tug and tow boats were often brought back into service.

Wootton and *Hilsea* were added to the service in 1928 and 1930 to meet the increase in motor car and lorry traffic. Motoring in the Isle of Wight, "drive on, drive off the new ferries," was popularised by posters on every railway station and elsewhere through the country, and traffic continued to increase. The three vessels were fully extended at summer week-ends, making 15 round trips on Saturdays. The two larger ships carried an average of 17/18 cars (or equivalent cars and lorries) per trip, the earlier smaller vessel taking 15/16 cars.

In 1961 a new terminal at Portsmouth and a new slipway at Fishbourne were built to meet the increasing traffic of private cars and goods deliveries to the Island by road vehicle in the post-war years. It is claimed that some holiday makers found no alternative but to take their cars over on Thursdays or Fridays, return to the mainland by passenger steamer and then take their families to the Island on Saturdays by the same means or face a holiday without a car!

One wonders whether it would not have been simpler and perhaps cheaper to have hired a car on reaching the Island, though of course travel fares and petrol were considerably cheaper then.

In 1969 and 1973 the *Cuthred* and *Caedmon* joined the fleet, both being larger vessels.

In 1972 a completely modernised terminal was opened at Fishbourne. The timber building constructed in 1926 was replaced by a cream brick building with a wooden fascia. It has a modern ticket office with a big window facing directly on to the road to enable motorists to purchase tickets without leaving their cars, a waiting room and refreshment rooms with a paved patio outside. There is a 10,700 square feet hard standing area for articulated lorry trailers, as well as a new car marshalling area with space for 300 cars. A one-way traffic system has been introduced to the new exit road leading to the main Ryde-Newport Road. The cost was £75,000.

With more new and larger ships being introduced on the route, this is a far cry from 1907 when barges holding three cars each brought over 30 cars a day. Today's vessels can operate in Force Ten wind conditions, winds of 48-55 nautical miles per hour, and they seldom have to stop for fog.

One ferryman who remembers the route in earlier days is Bert Butcher. He was a thirteen-year-old boy in 1914 when he walked down to Portsmouth

Point Beach to work the first of thousands of 16-hour a day hard slogs aboard the Solent's horse boats. He said "We had to work with the tide in the old days of tow-boats, and what I remember about those crossings—they took a good hour and a half—is the continual soakings because there was absolutely no shelter. We bought our own oilskins, we wore leather thigh boots (just think of it, leather boots in salt water) and we accepted that our travelling companions might be cattle, pigs, sheep, and the odd fellow human. The only thing that separated us from the animal cargo was a flimsy gate-type construction, . . . "

Fifty years ago a vehicle 15 feet in length would have been charged £2.14s. for the return trip, the driver paying 2s. 10d. (14.16 p) for his two-way crossing. A similar length vehicle would today be charged £11.40 with the driver paying £1.84.

The fleet of the Portsmouth and Ryde United Steam Packet Company was acquired by the L. & S.W. and L.B.S.C. Railway Companies in March 1880, passenger ferry services being operated by a joint committee of the two companies until the railway amalgamated in 1923, when Southern Railway took over. In 1948, when the railways were nationalised, railway vessels came under British Rail control.

At one period there was a weekly service from Brighton, but the name of the steamer is not known. The *Isle of Wight Observer* for July 1868 noted that 50 steamers arrived daily at Ryde pier head. At one stage Seaview, near Ryde, had a steam launch service from the mainland. Because the crossing was almost always rough it was known locally as the "sixpenny sick".

Seven paddle steamers were acquired by the two railway companies with others added from 1881 onwards. The *Duchess of Edinburgh* and *Duchess of Connaught,* built in 1884, each had a passenger complement of 551 compared with 426 on the previous vessel. These two ships were considered speedy and comfortable, with two first class saloons on the upper deck and two third class saloons on the main deck. They remained in service until 1910. As evidence of the increasing traffic on this route at that time six paddle steamers were introduced between 1889 and 1911. The *Duchess of Kent*, built in 1897, had a forward saloon and a full width promenade deck aft. The narrow after saloon was enclosed by alleyways on either side which became a distinctive feature of the Ryde fleet for many years. During the First World War she was engaged in war service as a mine sweeper. The *Duchess of Fife*, a similar though larger vessel, with accommodation for 838 passengers, operated for twenty years, and was also a mine sweeper during the War, while a number of other vessels on the route were engaged in war service of one kind or another.

The *Merston* and *Portsdown*, built in 1928, were different from other ships in the fleet by having enclosed wheelhouses and enclosed alleyways round the saloon aft and a large deck saloon amidships. *Portsdown* was blown up at Spithead in September 1941 during the Second World War, while taking the early mail service to Ryde. Most of the crew and passengers lost their lives in this episode.

Until the late years of the nineteenth century paddle ships were allowed to have paddles operated separately. However, a disaster to a pleasure steamer on the Thames occurred because passengers crowded to one side ready to disembark. In doing so they caused a list, with the paddles working independently, one going ahead, the other astern, with water locked in the paddle box. The list increased and the vessel capsized with great loss of life.

With these paddle steamers it was necessary to have a crew member on board at night to keep the steam up, and with the ever increasing cost of fuel and maintenance and the advent of twin-screw diesel vessels in 1948 and 1951 it was time to make a change and phase out the paddle steamers. 1969 therefore saw the end of these vessels which had operated over a period of more than a hundred and fifty years.

In 1948 a new generation of Portsmouth/Ryde passenger vessels entered the service. They were twin screw diesel vessels. At that time they were considered far superior to previous vessels in passenger comfort, speed and manoeuvrability with a capacity for well over one thousand passengers.

The record number of passengers conveyed on this route in one day, 67,645 on Saturday, 11th August 1956, is unlikely to be beaten, for passenger traffic to the Island by holiday makers in their own cars has meant a trans-

ı 1973 the Sealink ferry *Caedmon* on the Portsmouth to Fishbourne, Isle of Wight, crossing. *Sealink UK Limited*

ference from the passenger ferry to the car ferry. This, added to the competition of the local hovercraft service, has resulted in a significant decline in numbers availing themselves of the Portsmouth/Ryde service. This simply means that three vessels are now able to cope successfully, at all times, with the requirements of the service, which operates regularly throughout the day, the crossing taking 25 to 30 minutes.

Steam vessels first operated between **Southampton and Cowes** in 1820. Until that time the sailing vessels in use in the Solent made the journey slow and extremely tedious, especially in adverse weather conditions. When there was no wind the passage was made by rowing boats.

An instance is recorded of the captain having to abandon the use of the *Mermaid*, the regular sailing packet from Cowes to Southampton, and make the passage with the mail in a rowing boat in dead calm. Fog came on and after rowing until seven o'clock in the evening, and thinking they were near Southampton, they found themselves back in Cowes Harbour!

On 24th July 1820 the first steam vessel went into service on this route. This was five years earlier than a similar service started operating from Portsmouth to Ryde and ten years before the Lymington/Yarmouth route had its first steam vessel. This was the *Prince of Cobourg*, a small wooden hulled paddle wheel steam vessel of 52 tons, measuring only 76 feet 4½ inches in length, 14 feet 4½ inches in width and 5 feet 10 inches in depth of hold.

As with all early steamers she carried sails, having three masts and a bowsprit and a tall, thin funnel. Although most of the space below deck was taken up by the engine room, there was a small cabin forward for foredeck passengers and a state cabin aft for the use of those travelling first class. It was described as "elegantly fitted and very commodious." This boat made the voyage to Cowes and back three times a day, a distance of nearly 90 miles, part of which was against the wind and tide. It was recorded that her velocity in a calm against the tide was about eight knots.

Single fares were 2s. 6d. first class and 1s. 6d. in the fore cabin, whereas the fares by sailing boat were 1s. 6d. and 1s. A working man at that time might only be earning 10s. per week.

Other steam vessels quickly followed the *Cobourg* and two separate companies were established—the Isle of Wight Steam Packet Company, and the Isle of Wight Royal Mail Steam Packet Company. Unlike many other ferry operators who engaged in fierce competition, these two companies maintained the passage in harmony until 1861 when they became incorporated into one company claiming to have the longest title in the British Register of Companies—the Southampton Isle of Wight and South of England Royal Mail Steam Packet Company, popularly known as Red Funnel.

Paddle steamers were used exclusively until 1931 when the first twin screw diesel-engined vessel, the *Medina*, was introduced.

Today a regular service of three large, modern drive-through vehicle and passenger carrying motor vessels, nearly five times the size of the *Cobourg*, and more than twice as fast, make the direct passage between Southampton and West and East Cowes in fifty minutes. These vessels are the *Norris Castle, Cowes Castle* and *Netley Castle*. They are designed to meet the specific requirements of this service, and can accommodate the largest commercial vehicles. Access is over wide ramps through bow and stern doors and special mezzanine decks allow vehicles to be double parked during the peak holiday season. Each vessel can carry up to 90 cars and 950 passengers. Large observation lounges on the promenade deck extend the full width of the vessels, with extra large windows giving passengers an unimpaired view while seated. Full refreshment facilities are available on board.

A comparatively recent innovation is the Hydrofoil. The *Shearwater,* which was put into service in May 1969, makes the journey in approximately twenty minutes. The hull is kept well above the water by means of skis or foils which automatically adjust to the speed of the craft, giving a faster "take off" than other hydrofoils, with the craft becoming "foil-borne" quicker.

Shearwater 2 was added to the service at the end of July 1970 to improve the reliability of the service, and extensive modifications were made to the pontoon at West Cowes to improve berthing facilities. In 1973 larger "second generation" Hydrofoils, *Shearwater 3* and *4* each seating 67 passengers, took over and have proved a great success with commuters and holiday makers alike.

Red Funnel claim to carry more passengers, vehicles and freight to and from Southampton than any other shipping line using the port. In 1978 the totals were over half a million passengers, 160,000 cars, 58,000 commercial vehicles and 197,000 tons of freight.

Services are arranged to allow deliveries to be made to the Island and to return to the mainland the same day.

The Cowes Floating Bridge, between **East and West Cowes**, a vehicular and passenger ferry, saves a journey of 10 miles via Newport.

The Royal Ferry rights across the River Medina at Cowes were held by John Robertson of West Cowes, who sold them to the Floating Bridge Company in 1859. This Company sold them to the Steam Packet Company, now Red Funnel Steamers Limited, in 1868, and in 1901 an Act of Parliament was passed enabling the two Councils of East and West Cowes to take over the operation of the ferry. In 1972 it was taken over by the Isle of Wight County Council, its present owners.

The ferry was originally steam engine operated, but in 1936 diesel electric machinery was fitted to a new ferry, since when the steam engined ferries have been replaced by diesels. The last vessel to come into service, in May 1976, is diesel hydraulic propelled.

The ferry now operates on two one and half inch diagonal long link high tensile steel chains, each 180 yards long.

Local people with relatives on the other side of the river use the ferry, also holiday makers wishing to go to Osborne House, but the main passengers are workmen from the British Hovercraft factory.

The ferry operates about every ten minutes, seven days a week, every day of the year including Christmas, starting at 5.30 a.m. (Sundays 7 a.m.) and finishing at 11.20 p.m., which averages 200 trips a day. In the year ended 1976, 159,000 children's tickets were sold, 693,000 adults', and 31,000 adult weekly tickets. 170,000 cars and 6,000 lorries used the service during the same period.

In 1936 a pair of chains cost £178, while today they cost £3,200 and their average life is 30 to 36 months. This has involved a considerable increase in tolls charged today as compared with the halfpenny and penny fares of 1901, but, without the ferry, traffic would have to spend more time and money on making the detour around Newport.

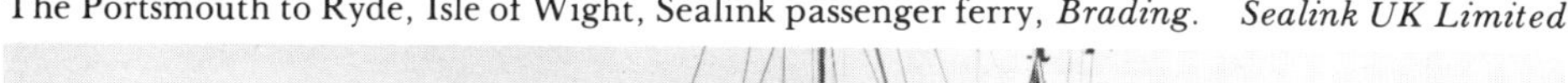

The Portsmouth to Ryde, Isle of Wight, Sealink passenger ferry, *Brading*. *Sealink UK Limited*

CHAPTER FIVE

Canal and Lakeland

BEFORE the Manchester Ship Canal was constructed there were ferries across the River Mersey at points approximately where the **Bobs Lane** and **Thelwell Ferries** are at the present time. A condition imposed on the canal constructors was that wherever a road was bisected a bridge or ferry must provide a crossing.

There was doubtless a bridge of some kind in the vicinity of **Hulmes Ferry** because this was originally known as Holmes Bridge Ferry.

With the exception of **Irlam Passenger Ferry**, those now in use have been operating since the Ship Canal was opened in 1894. These are passenger ferries but they also carry bicycles and perambulators at an increased fare.

Hulmes Ferry, which is just over a mile below Barton High Level Bridge, is still used by people passing between Davyhulme and Irlam. It is a free ferry operating from 6 a.m. until midnight and can carry a maximum of 14 passengers.

Until 1966 Irlam Ferry was a vehicular ferry using a pontoon for carrying vehicles and also a boat for pedestrians. The passenger ferry operated across the Canal just above Irlam Locks and about a mile below Hulmes Ferry. It was open day and night and used by people passing between Flixton, Urmston and Irlam. It carried a maximum of 18 passengers, the single fare being 1d. per person, 2d. with bicycle or perambulator. Weekly fares were 8d. and 1s. 4d. respectively.

Following discussions with the two local authorities mainly concerned, Urban District Councils of Irlam and Urmston, the Canal Company was relieved of its obligation to provide a vehicular ferry, but they did agree to provide a new motorised ferry for pedestrians and cyclists.

At 12.30 p.m. on 15th May 1968 the new passenger ferry was formally opened. The two Councils each contributed £500 a year towards the provision and upkeep of the ferry, though this contribution and the fares set were to be the subject of review in the light of experience both of running costs and the number of passengers carried. The total cost to the Canal Company in providing the ferry and landing stages amounted to approximately £30,000, which was substantially more than was envisaged when the charges and contributions were first agreed. This new ferry also carried invalid carriages, mopeds and motor cycles which were too small to use the M62. Fares were increased to 3d. for each single journey and a further 3d. for each vehicle, with children under three travelling free.

Named *Traverse*, and accommodating twenty passengers, the new boat was fitted with twin jet propulsion units and was 30 feet long by 12 feet wide. It was specially designed to operate in all weather with particular emphasis on manoeuvrability, safety and ease of access.

However, operating costs continued to rise and it became evident about six years later that if the ferry was to continue at all the Company would be entitled to an enormous increase in the fares or in the subsidy from the local authorities, probably both. The parties concerned therefore decided to discontinue the ferry and provide a walkway for public use over Irlam Locks. The work of resurfacing the approach roads and the fitting of suitable platforms on top of the lock gates for public use was undertaken by the Manchester Ship Canal Company, and the cost of maintenance is now shared between the Company and the highway authority, which is the Greater Manchester Council.

The other crossing which should be mentioned is Bob's Lane Ferry, which operates between Partington and Irlam. This was a strictly private venture run by the ferryman using a rowing boat with outboard motor, but in order to make it a viable proposition the Canal Company subsidised it.

In 1974, when the ferry was operating at a loss, a final effort to make it viable was made by the introduction of a new modern steel-hulled launch, the MSC *Cadishead*. The vessel was brought into service to operate between Partington and Irlam, replacing the existing boat. The new launch was 30 feet long and powered by a 25 horse-power Lister engine. It was specially designed for the job and equipped to the highest standards of safety. Seating accommodation for twelve passengers was provided in an enclosed cabin with a space at the rear for prams and bicycles. The passenger fare was increased from 2½d. to 3d. for adults for each single journey, and 2½d. for children under fourteen years of age.

From 1976 the ferry has been running under the management and at the cost of the G.M.C., the ferryboat being renamed the *G.M.C. Cadishead*. Until the take-over in 1976 the local authorities had, in varying degrees, subsidised the operation of the ferry from 1972.

The Company also operates a number of ferries which are not available to the general public.

Lakeland

For well over a hundred years Lakeland communities have been served by a variety of vessels operating a regular service between lakeside townships and villages such as **Windermere** and **Coniston.**

The Furness Railway Steam Yacht *Swift* arriving at Ambleside Pier. The Railway ran steamers on both Windermere and Coniston Lakes.

Transport began before the era of steam, the boats employed functioning mainly as ferries across the water and not as pleasure conveyances except in a limited degree. Until 1845 the only regular communication along the lake was by passenger boats run by White & Gibson of **Ambleside**, connecting with the Ulverston and Lancaster coaches by **Newby Bridge.**

Windermere is the largest lake in England and is just over ten miles long. It is 285 feet at its deepest at the northern end of the lake and one mile wide at the widest point.

Oar-propelled barges, assisted by sail, were used before the introduction of steam. They were operated by an Ambleside firm to work as ferries between

Ambleside at the northern end of Lake Windermere and Newby Bridge in the south and were timed to connect with the horse-drawn coach service between Ulverston and Lancaster. The journey took up to three and a half hours.

In 1825 Windermere Steam Yacht Company was formed. This Company ordered a wooden steamer from Richard Ashburner, who later founded the first ship-building yard at Barrow-in-Furness. Named the *Lady of the Lake* she was launched on 26th July 1845 from a slip close by the *Swan Hotel* at Newby Bridge.

Originally she was fitted with a figure-head and two masts, which later had to be removed because they became entangled with trees in the half mile stretch between the open lake and the landing stage at Newby Bridge. But she had a mixed reception; landowners feared the amenities of the lake would be affected by the ferry belching smoke from its funnel and that herds of trippers would interfere with the peace of the place; others, more dependent on the ferry service, welcomed this new form of transport. She had a length of 80 feet with a beam of 11 feet 6 inches and a depth of 6 feet 4 inches and could carry 200 people. She was an immediate success, in the first short season carrying more than 5,000 passengers.

However, in May 1861 she sprang a leak. The vessel began to sink and the Ambleside ferryman was signalled by the ship's steam whistle, but some of the passengers panicked and jumped into the lake. The remainder were taken off by the Ambleside Ferry.

The success of the Steam Yacht Company brought a competitor to the scene—the Windermere Iron Steam Boat Company—which began to operate in 1849 with an iron paddle steamer named *Fire Fly*. The next year this new company launched the *Dragon Fly*, a larger vessel. This was followed by fierce competition between the two companies, with fare slashing and noisy touting for custom at the piers. By 1856 a working agreement was reached and two years later the two companies were merged in the Windermere United Steam Yacht Company.

This united company launched the *Swan* five days after the opening of Lakeside Station. This vessel operated for sixty-eight summers but on more than one occasion she was sunk and was raised without serious damage. Finally, on a foggy day in 1909, she ran ashore on the western side of the lake.

Today Sealink U.K. Limited operate on Lake Windermere. This is the smallest of the Sealink Fleets but it has consistently shown a profit. Four diesel-engined twin-screw ferries operate, the *Swift, Swan, Tern* and *Teal*, the *Swan* and *Teal* being the bigger boats. They are fitted with V.H.F. radio and tannoy and can carry 625 passengers. When I was there, on a very wet and misty day towards the end of August 1977, 200 passengers were on board the *Swan*.

Local demand, though dependent on the ferry service, is small compared with the tourist traffic in the season. The basic service is between Lake Side,

Bowness and Ambleside. An average of 750,000 passengers a year are carried on the four vessels in a five-month period of sailing.

The crew are justly proud of the fact that the ferry service has only been suspended on six days since 1970 and on each occasion it was because of high winds.

Master, crew and administrative staff take their holidays after sailing finishes. During the summer they work a seven day week with a day off once a fortnight. The two big vessels are on duty from 8 a.m. until 6.30 p.m. The engineer on the *Swan* told me he has served on the Windermere Ferries for thirty-one years. Docking and maintenance is carried out personally by masters and crews in the short days of winter which is doubtless why these ferries have been in operation for so many years.

Queen Elizabeth II travelled on the *Teal* in August 1956 on her passage from Ambleside to Bowness.

The *Teal,* a diesel-engined ferry of Sealink's smallest fleet, on Lake Windermere.

CHAPTER SIX

Scottish Ferries

THE great cities of the world have, in general, achieved greatness by their accessibility to the sea. Glasgow is one such city and **Clyde River Ferries** have played their part in achieving this. There were many cross river ferries operating on the Clyde in the early years of the nineteenth century, while vessels known as Cluthas (Clutha being the Gaelic name for Clyde) maintained a down-river service. In those days the coastal resorts on the lower reaches of the Clyde were served by steam boats, the railways having been unsuccessful in their efforts to compete. The fierce opposition from the steamship owners with their lower fares was against them.

Forty river steamers, operated by a dozen different owners, were running in 1888. They were not all strictly ferries, of course, but are indicative of the amount of river traffic at that time and of the fact that it had become necessary for the smaller companies to amalgamate or go out of business.

Until then, and for some years earlier, no passenger vessel had been allowed to ply on the river on Sundays. There was more than a religious reason for this for, in the mid-Victorian years, the sale of intoxicating liquor was forbidden on Sundays. The steamer *Victoria* broke that law with an excursion service on Sundays, during which her passengers were drinking on board liquor they could not obtain ashore. Local inhabitants of the coastal towns where the ferry stopped were naturally angry when "herds of savages and drunken rabbles" shattered the peace of their Sundays. In 1897 Bye-law No. 5 was submitted by the Dunoon Commissioners for the approval of the Board of Trade. It read:-

> "No steamer or other vessel shall be permitted to land or embark passengers at the pier between 12 midnight on Saturdays and 12 midnight on Sunday without the special sanction of the Commissioners, under a penalty by the party or parties in charge of the said steamer or other vessel of a sum not exceeding £5 for each passenger landed or embarked in contravention thereof."

While the Bye-law was under discussion efforts were made to keep the Sunday river traffic operating. Feelings ran high, with crowds of 12,000 people waiting at the pier gates and angry scenes when they clashed with the police.

The old *Clansman* was also a Royal Mail Ship. The present Caledonian MacBrayne *Clansman* was built in 1964 and converted in 1973.

Eventually the Bye-law was passed but the debate continued until the end of 1901 when Sunday sailings with landings at the pier were permitted. I was told there still were some places in the Highlands of Scotland where no Sunday service runs. When travelling on the ferries in 1977, I was advised that if I took the ferry from **Stornaway to Ullapool** on Saturday I would not be able to travel on many of the ferries in Skye the next day, though actually I did find the **Kyleakin Ferry** operating then.

In 1848 the Clyde Navigation Trust, formed in 1809 to manage the affairs of Glasgow Harbour, took over the lease of three existing ferries which had been run by private operators. From that time ten places along the river were provided with a ferry service by the Trust or other agencies, the craft varying through the years from rowing boats to steam-driven vessels. Steam vessels were introduced in 1864, after a boat had over-turned in the previous year with 19 men being drowned. In later years boats were diesel-driven.

During 1872 seven million passengers crossed the river. In the next thirteen years traffic had grown to such an extent that nine million passengers and a quarter of a million vehicles were making the crossing each year. Fares were abolished on all routes on the upper reaches of the river in 1920, leaving only two ferries which were charging tolls. Although these ferries had provided a very useful service, the development of modern road transport created a need for bridges and tunnels over and under the river, and the ferries gradually faded out.

The opening of the Glasgow Subway Railway, and later the introduction of the Corporation's tramcars going west through districts along both sides of the river, led to a steady decline in the service which had transported millions of passengers down the river over many years.

Many have heard of the MacBrayne Ferries, now known as **Caledonian MacBrayne Ferries**. "MacBrayne's is unique", was a statement made by John Purdie in an article in *Scottish Field* in November 1968. The writer went on to explain that, although the Company, with its 800 employees, is only a medium-sized concern in U.K. terms, it is a very large company in Highland terms. It is unique because it is the part property of every U.K. taxpayer and also the very intimate property of most of the people who live north of the Highland line. John Purdie describes MacBraynes as "the Government instrument for the provision of sea services on the waters between the west of Scotland and the Hebrides, and of bus services in the area. The purpose of the company is to provide a service which could only be classified as meeting a social need," which is why the Government subsidises it.

Although it might be thought the **Highlands and Islands Ferries**, which cross the sea, sometimes for considerable distances, do not rightly belong to a book on river ferries, they are such an essential part of, and so necessary to the life of the people of Scotland, that it seems right to include them here.

In 1891 the Glasgow and South Western Railway obtained Parliamentary powers to run steamers, and retained their interest in the service until 1948 when, with the nationalisation of the Railways, their fleets amalgamated under the British Transport Commission. Fifty per cent of the holding was with David MacBrayne Ltd., which Company was also transferred to the British Transport Commission. However, nine years later all railway controlled vessels were transferred to the Caledonian Steam Packet Company (C.S.P.). In 1973 the C.S.P. and David MacBrayne Limited amalgamated to form Caledonian MacBrayne Limited with control of the combined fleet, which is quite considerable, more than twenty vessels being in operation today.

The *Juno*, on which I travelled from **Gourock** across the Clyde to Dunoon and back, at the end of August 1977, is capable of conveying 40 cars and 674 passengers. During peak periods the average number of passengers is 300 on each trip. Every morning workers cross on this vessel to go to the Royal Ordnance Factory at Kilcreggan. The first crossing from Gourock is at 6.45 a.m., returning from Dunoon at 7.25 a.m. The last ferry of the day leaves Gourock for Dunoon at 8.45 p.m., the return being made at 9.15 p.m., except on Fridays and Saturdays when there is a ferry at 10.30 p.m. The *Juno* has been in service on this crossing in company with the *Jupiter*, since December

Originally the *Cygnus* had a clipper bow and two tall funnels. She ran between Weymouth and the Channel Islands from 1857 to 1899 and then between Liverpool and the Isle of Man. Bought by MacBrayne she was put in hand for alterations in 1892 and emerged renamed *Brigadier*. Principal changes involved a new swan bow and a single funnel before operating on the Oban-Loch Sunart station and the Outer Islands service from Portree. This paddle steamer was wrecked on Duncan's Rock, Near Rodel, Harris on 7th December 1896.

Courtesy of the Oban Times

1974. Both vessels are fitted with Voith-Schneider propellers. The *Juno's* measurements are—length 227 feet, breadth 45 feet and she has a gross tonnage of 854. One of the improvements which has been incorporated in this vessel is the flying bridge above the navigational bridge, giving her captain an unrestricted view aft. Her speed is 12 knots, the crossing takes 20 minutes with 10 minutes at the pier at each end. The crew consists of the master, mate, three seamen, chief engineer, second engineer and purser. There is a barman and messroom boy.

The *Glen Sannox*, built specifically for the Arran route, with a speed of over 18 knots, was the fastest post-war vessel in the fleet. Most vessels are moved from time to time to different routes especially in the winter months. The *Glen Sannox* was no exception. This larger and more powerful vessel operated the Gourock to Dunoon service from November 1971 until March 1974, at which time the *Jupiter* came into use.

When I crossed from **Wemyss Bay to Rothesay** at the beginning of September 1977, the *Glen Sannox* was in operation there. She had arrived in May of that year to inaugurate the roll-on roll-off terminals and was to remain until the next addition to the fleet arrived. She had stern-loading with capacity for more than 1,000 passengers and 64 cars or 40 cars and 8 lorries, though when running from **Oban to Glasgow** with the longer sea route, she was only permitted to take 858 passengers. For the past two years the Wemyss Bay to Rothesay Ferry has been taking men out to Ardyne Point to work on the oil rig.

When *Glen Sannox* was commissioned in 1957, the cargo service ceased. cars were transported by one of the side-loading ferries about three times a week.

Experiments were made with a hovercraft on this route, but it cost twice as much as the normal ferry and only carried 60 passengers. The steamer speed on this route is 16 knots, the crossing taking half an hour.

There is a good waiting room at Rothesay which was opened by the Queen Mother in 1968. This was an amenity I missed on a number of other ferry routes.

In June 1971 far reaching proposals for the traffic to **Cumbrae** were announced. Slipways were to be built at Largs and at the Cumbrae Slip and a small, bow-loader was to be employed on the service. The new service was inaugurated in March 1972. After some initial problems, including opposition from Millport Town Council, traffic increased until, at peak periods, a ten-minute, three-ship service was needed.

But everything did not work smoothly. Breakdowns were numerous and delays frequent. A larger, purpose-built ship was required and the *Isle of Cumbrae*, a new vessel, was brought into use on 1st April 1977 for the Largs to Cumbrae Slip crossing. Cumbrae Slip had been extended and widened considerably and the area round the slip at Largs dredged.

This new ship has a gross tonnage of 201 and her dimensions are—length 125 feet, breadth 33 feet and draught of 4 feet 5 inches. She is a flat-bottomed steel vessel with carrying capacity for 160 passengers together with 15 cars. Her name—*Isle of Cumbrae*— was chosen by competition among Millport school children.

Now the people of Cumbrae and Millport are well served with a much more reliable service, so important to them in their isolated position.

The crossing from **Ardrossan to Brodick** is well known to tourists visiting the Isle of Arran. Since 20th April 1976 the *Clansman* has been making five or more daily crossings between these two places. Captain McLean, the master on this vessel when I crossed in August 1977, was not the only one who spoke of the problems created with the ship catching the wind because of the additional height of this modern ferry, especially when operating in restricted harbours in bad weather. The *Clansman's* length is 266 feet, breadth 46 feet and draught 9 feet 1 inch, with gross tonnage of 1,707. She carries a maximum of 870 passengers and 50 cars. Built in 1964, with roll-on roll-off, the height is necessary for the car deck to be accommodated. The draught cannot be altered because of the piers which have to be worked. In winter the *Caledonia* takes over. She is a smaller ship with considerably less tonnage and less carrying capacity.

When the *Clansman* was first put into service she was the relief ship of the fleet, going wherever her services were required. Every Friday evening, between June and September, from 1967, she had made the long voyage to Lochboisdale, returning during the night in time to take her place on the Skye sailing schedule on the Saturday. In 1971 and 1972 she took in Barra as well, making the journey three times a week.

She had a most unusual task when, in January 1969, she was moored in the Thames at Tower Pier to house the Highland Fling exhibition staged by the Highlands and Islands Development Board. The exhibitions attracted 40,000 visitors.

Major alterations were made to the *Clansman* at Troon where she remained for nine months, from October 1972. She was cut in two just forward of the funnel and her length extended by 36 feet. Her passenger accommodation was raised by 3 feet forward and 5 feet aft and she was fitted with a bow visor and stern door. Her hoist was removed and filled in, which gave a good open deck-end forward of the passenger lounges. As a final touch she was fitted with two new masts. By the end of June 1973 she was ready to replace the *Iona* on the **Ullapool to Stornaway** run. This was a good example of what can be done to a ship, for I was told she was scarcely recognisable when the alterations were completed.

In the course of my travels I have seen a hydrofoil undergoing a similar operation. I crossed from Ardrossan to Brodick a year after the *Clansman* had

The MacBrayne vessel *Hebrides* approaches the North Pier at Oban. *Courtesy of the Oban Times*

her extension completed and found her a fine ship, but I did not see her in her former size. She now does five or more daily crossings on that ferry.

In Oban I was met by Mr Mackenzie, the Area Manager, who came into the service forty years ago. It was a misty, wet morning when I made the trip from **Oban to Mull**. With strong currents at certain states of the tide the crossing can be very rough.

The ferry runs to Mull six times a day in summer and four times on Sundays. In winter there are only three ferry services a day and none on Sundays. There is no hospital on Mull and, in emergencies, one of MacBrayne's small ferries provides an emergency service from Craigavie to Oban.

We were making the crossing on the *Columba*, which is described as the most famous of the MacBrayne steamers of all time, although this is the third ship of that name. The first *Columba* sailed from **Glasgow to Ardrishaig** almost every summer from 1878 until 1935. The survival of the name in 1964 was justifiably greeted with enthusiasm.

With dimensions of 235 feet × 46 feet × 9 feet, and a gross tonnage of 1,420, her maximum passenger complement is 600 with 50 cars. From July

1964 until 1973 she was engaged on the crossing between Oban and Mull. Craignure had recently become the main port for Mull, her pier having been opened to traffic in December 1963. There is a link span for stern loading.

July and August are the peak periods, especially at week-ends. Mull is a great attraction for tourists with its overland route to Iona.

The *Columba*, like many others in the service, is fitted with automatic steering, 2 radars, radio telephone and, in fact, all modern aids.

The starting of the car ferry in 1964 resulted in a 300 per cent increase in traffic, which has now levelled off, but still people who do not book ahead for the seasonal ferries may be left behind at week-ends.

Captain Gunn and James West, the first officer, told me how dependent the people on **Lismore and Mull** are on the two ferries which ply regularly back and forth between these islands. Lismore is 12 miles long and has a small farming population. They, like most of the people on the small islands, need the ferry for their domestic supplies and also for the transport of their stock and produce.

From 1972 this ferry has been used extensively for the transport of livestock and may take as many as 240 lambs and 200 sheep, or up to 90 head of cattle, depending on their size. For this purpose the *Columba* also calls at the Outer Isles.

One of the most popular of the annual Highland Gatherings, the Tobermory Games, takes place in July and from 1969 the ferry has been calling there specially on these occasions.

There was some local opposition when Sunday sailings started in 1972, the ferry service being combined with short cruises to different places, but apparently that was overcome, for these Sunday services still operate. In fact, in May 1975, this idea of combining excursions with ferry sailings was extended, and the *Columba* now makes four excursions a week to **Coll and Tiree,** three to **Colonsay** and two to **Iona**. Mini cruises, with passengers using the ship as a floating hotel for two or three days while touring the Isles, also proved successful and of financial assistance. Many ferries in other parts of Great Britain find this enables a satisfactory ferry service to be maintained.

During the winter months there is the usual turn around of ships while some are laid off for renovations and repairs and for inspection for their D.o.T. certificates.

A group of ferries known as Small Island Class Vessels started operating in 1972. The first two were bow-loading ferries each capable of carrying five cars and about fifty passengers who were accommodated in a deck shelter aft. The *Raasay* was the last of the fleet of eight, coming into service in April 1976. They act as a lifeline to small communities. When I was on the ferry going to Mull the Captain told me that one of these Island Class vessels had been chartered by a man who owned an island and wanted to move a house-ful of furniture from the mainland. The job was completed in less than three hours, a loaded furniture van being put on the ship and landed at the other end. As soon as the furniture was unloaded the Small Island Ferry returned to the mainland with the empty van.

The **Treshmish Isles** are one of the groups served by landing class boats. Ramps with wooden barriers are put down for the loading of animals going to the October sales, all the larger cattle coming in on one day and medium-sized cattle the following day.

On another wet and misty morning I boarded the *Iona* for the trip from **Oban to Lochboisdale.** Captain Angus Campbell told me he had started with the Company in 1948 as second mate, later become first mate and finally skipper. It was to be a six-hour journey to Lochboisdale but owing to the bad weather which had prevailed for the last two hours, the *Iona* was running late. When we did depart the Captain told me of an occasion in 1969 when storm force winds kept his ship in port at Tiree for twenty-four hours. She could not lift off the pier until the wind died away on the following day. She was bound for **Barra** and Lochboisdale with 40 passengers, and there was no sleeping accommodation. The Company had to feed the passengers and they bedded down on blankets. The pressure of wind was so strong that it hove the anchor in.

After that story I felt we were fortunate to be only two hours late arriving at Lochboisdale, but I heard later that the *Iona*, though due to make the return journey to Oban the next morning, could not sail until the following day.

Captain Campbell also remembered the time when cattle and other livestock were transported to the ship in boxes and put on by derrick. On Skye the cattle swam ashore but sheep were put on small boats and rowed in.

As we neared Lochaline we looked to see whether a flag had been hoisted as a signal that we were needed to pick up there. Since we were running late the Captain was relieved that no flag was flying. We saw two lighthouses in the distance during the journey, Lismore, which has an automatic light, and Ardnemurchen, the most westerly lighthouse on the British mainland.

The *Iona*, a new large dual-purpose ferry, was launched on 22nd January 1970, making her first passenger sailing on 29th May of that year between Gourock and Dunoon where she remained until November 1971, using the end loading terminal at Gourock from July 1971. It was not until 29th April 1974 that she started a new fast daily "Marine Motorway" from Oban to Barra and Lochboisdale. Her dimensions when built in 1970 were 244 feet × 46 feet × 10 feet, with a gross tonnage of 1,192 and capacity for 349 passengers and 47 cars, but in 1975 she was refitted with a new deckhouse with eight cabins on the upper deck aft of the officers' accommodation.

Like most other vessels on these ferry routes, the *Iona* has been moved around until there is hardly a pier or drive-on drive-off terminal in the Clyde or West Highlands she has not visited, although now she seems to have found her place in the network of services in the isles.

In 1945 the London Midland and Scottish Railway (L.M.S.) took control of the Skye Ferry service from **Kyleaken to Lochalsh** when three turntable ferries and a motor launch were operating, but bigger and better boats became necessary as motor traffic increased in the 1950s and 60s. Both the British Transport Commission and the C.S.P., who were successive owners, commissioned more ferries, but even so queues of cars built up, some having to wait for four hours to make the four-minute crossing. When the Scottish Transport Group took over the service they commissioned two large end-loading ferries to carry 28 cars. These were named the *Kyleakin* and the *Lochalsh*. Both ships were identical apart from the arrangement of their masts. They were equipped with Voith-Schneider propellers fore and aft which makes them extremely manoeuvrable. These replaced the turntables previously in use. They are flat-bottomed boats with diesel engines, and can take any length of vehicle. Lorry drivers stay in their vehicles but passengers in

The Caledonian MacBrayne's *Columba* at Craignure in October, 1971. *Courtesy of the Oban Times*

coaches and private cars join the foot passengers on deck. This is normal on ferries.

The peak season only lasts for four weeks—from the middle of July until the middle of August. This had just finished when I was there and only one ferry was running, but it was making the return journey very quickly, leaving the pier every 20 minutes, and it was going back and forth with passengers and cars continuously. In winter the ferry runs approximately every half hour.

The Department of Trade survey takes place every year and the overhaul can take at least two months.

Fares in 1977 were 10p for passengers and £1. 15 for cars. Commercial vehicles and coaches pay 74p per metre plus V.A.T. on commercial vehicles.

The service starts at 5.30 a.m. on weekdays with the last ferry running at 11.25 p.m. This applies summer and winter alike, on summer Sundays the timing is 10 a.m. until 9 p.m. and in winter 10 a.m. until 5.30 p.m.

In his book, *Skye—The Island and its Legends*, Otta Swire recalls the early days on this ferry when it consisted of "two planks laid across a row-boat. On to those planks, with care and skill, and at certain states of the tide only, the car must be driven; then it was made fast with ropes through the wheel spokes. If it was a calm day all was well, but if the centre of the kyle was choppy, and it often is choppy from the point of view of a rowing-boat, there came the awful moment for the car owner when the ropes were cast off with the ominous words:- 'If she (the boat) rolls too much now, she (the car) will just slip off and maybe not sink us?'"

Nevertheless, added the writer, "though it looked and sounded alarming I never saw a car 'slip off' and only heard of one being lost. The ferrymen knew their job well."

I think the most exciting and interesting day I had on these Scottish ferries was that spent on the tour of the Small Islands. I seemed to be destined to have rain and wind for a great deal of the time while I was in Scotland on this occasion, but none worse than on the day appointed for this trip. I had travelled down by coach from Kyleakin to **Armadale**—a long ride with a full coachload. We were within a couple of miles or so of the starting point for the ferry when the coach broke down. The coach driver apologised but said he was going to hitch a lift to get some assistance! For half an hour we sat in the coach—at least some of us did, some of the hardier among us braved the elements and set out to walk to the ferry. It seemed certain we would miss the ferry as we constantly checked our watches and looked anxiously down the road, until the relief coach arrived and the driver assured us we would reach our destination in time. We did. The elements had played their part in delaying tactics and the ship, the *Bute*, was only just unloading vehicles at Armadale when we reached there. The rain had ceased but it was still very windy. The assembly point was packed with vehicles of all kinds and it looked

The Hebridean ferry *Loch Seaforth* at Mallaig during 1970. *S. J. Boothman*

as though we would have a full load of vehicles and passengers. The *Bute* is equipped with turntable and side-loading, which caused further delay in getting all vehicles aboard.

We were 45 minutes late leaving Armadale for the four and a half mile, half-hour crossing to Mallaig, but Captain Callender, Master of the *Bute*, assured me the boat for the Small Isles would wait. Asked why, with so much traffic, they were using a vessel with side-loading, he explained that it would be too costly to build link spans at Mallaig and at Armadale for a summer only trade, to widen the approach roads, adapt the port facilities to cope with the additional traffic and provide suitable docking for end-loading.

The *Bute* is one of the first three car ferries built for the West Coast of Scotland. Built at Troon in 1954, she has capacity for 650 passengers and 30 cars, or a lesser number when caravans and buses are included. Her dimensions are 185 feet × 35 feet × 7 feet 6 inches, and she has a gross tonnage of 568. In 1955 she actually transported the contents of a farm from Brodick to Ayr! She only serves the **Armadale to Mallaig** crossing from May until September, and does not run on Sundays. Starting from Mallaig at 8.15 in the morning she returns from Armadale at 9.15 a.m., and this continues throughout the day although weather can upset the time-table, as I found, as can distress calls which happen occasionally, particularly with small boats and yachts in distress. Such a call had been made that morning from the northern end of Skye.

The rain had started again and there was a gale force wind when I met Mr McGillivray, the Port Officer at Mallaig. I was rather hesitant about taking this trip in such conditions, especially when, on enquiry, it was confirmed that the vessel used for the Small Islands had no stablisers. The Captain of the *Bute* had been reassuring as was the Port Officer, but I was still concerned about being an embarrassment with sea sickness. In the event all was well and I would have been more than sorry to have missed such a trip.

The *Bute* arrived at 1.10 p.m. and the *Loch Arkaig* left almost immediately for Eigg, Rhum, Canna and Mallaig, a round trip scheduled to take six hours. Built of wood in 1941 by John Bolson of Poole, as an inshore mine sweeper, the *Loch Arkaig* joined the MacBrayne fleet in 1959 going direct to the Clyde where she was stripped of her original fittings. She was given new Bergius engines which drove her at around 11 knots, and steel bulkheads and superstructure. Following her refit she started her new career as a passenger and cargo ship on 14th April 1960. When calling at Raasay, which did not have an extensive road network, the odd car which travelled on the ferry had to be run aboard on planks at suitable states of the tide.

When MacBrayne inaugurated their car ferries in 1964 the *Loch Arkaig* was fitted with a ferry door on the starboard side of the lounge and a samson post and derrick forward to make the handling of cargo easier. She then became a lifeline to the small islands, sailing from Mallaig on five days a week in summer, and making four trips a week in winter, filling in other times with some excursions.

The *Loch Arkaig* is a small vessel, her dimensions being 117 feet × 22 feet × 8 feet 1 inch. Her gross tonnage is 179. **Canna** is the only one of the Small Isles to boast a pier. At **Eigg, Muck and Rhum** passengers, cargo and livestock have to be ferried ashore. This, and the very exposed nature of the crossing, has made it difficult to design a suitable replacement for this old wooden ship. Because of the uneconomic nature of the service to these sparsely populated islands, the Government subsidy required is administered separately and the *Loch Arkaig* is still owned by David MacBrayne Ltd., as distinct from Caledonian MacBrayne.

The Master and Chief Engineer work three weeks on and three weeks off in summer with a fortnight on and fortnight off in winter. The mates and second engineer work a fortnight on and fortnight off all through the year.

Obviously no vehicles can be taken on this trip but bicycles and motor cycles are transported. The population of these islands is very small—about 16 at Canna, 18 at Muck and 25 to 35 at Rhum. Tourists visit them in the summer months and groups of geologists and university students stay on the islands for field studies at different times.

As we approached Eigg a small ferry filled with young people came across from the island. There were twenty with four tutors. The boat was loaded with tents, rucksacks and island produce. Passengers boarded the *Loch Arkaig* with the help of the crew, while the small boat rocked on the stormy sea. When their baggage had been taken on board the cargo we had brought for the island had to be off-loaded on to the small boat. This included cartons of domestic supplies, bags of feeding stuff from Greenock or Portree and some mail.

The young people were very excited and friendly as they settled in the cafeteria with cups of tea and snacks. They had responded to a programme put out on Yorkshire Television to go on an expedition to Eigg and engage in an adventure course for two weeks. Walking, swimming, studying geology, plants, animals and birds, making notes of what they found and keeping a log book seemed to have occupied their two weeks very happily. The youngest was a bright twelve year old and the eldest eighteen-and-a-half. The went to Eigg on the *Shearwater*, a small harbour craft which can go right in to the pier. They would have returned on the same boat but the sea was too rough for her to moor.

They told me that there are eighty people living on this island which has a small school with eight children. There is only one main road, three guest houses and two churches, one the Church of Scotland and the other Roman Catholic. There is a post office, an automatic telephone exchange and a tea shop. All this I learned from the young people who produced their log books as cups slid about on the tables, occasionally falling on to the floor. They seemed to have found their adventure great fun even when their big tent had blown down, the ridge pole having broken while they were still in bed that morning, and the cook tent had caught fire!

Caledonian MacBrayne's *Pioneer* on trials during August, 1974. *Courtesy of the Oban Times*

Cars loading at South Ballachulish to cross Loch Leven to North Ballachulish in 1973 whilst bridge building was in progress. *S. J. Boothman*

We stopped briefly outside the other Islands on the route. A fishing boat brought out a few passengers and packages from one island. There is a small ferry at Rhum operated by two local men, but Caledonian MacBrayne maintain it. This is the *Four Winds* which came out with a few passengers, some mail and a good deal of luggage and rucksacks. A bundle of car tyres, crates of tomatoes, eggs, cabbage and sacks of potatoes were also transferred to the *Loch Arkaig*.

While huge breakers washed against the vessel the Captain told me that only on very few occasions have they been unable to sail because of weather, and that mainly in the winter.

Lorne Campbell, the author, is the popular landlord on Canna who looks after his workers. Their small fishing vessel can carry 20 sheep and red deer are also exported from Rhum. The *Loch Arkaig* does not take animals but I could imagine the confusion which would arise if animals were transferred to our vessel in midstream!

The Nature Conservancy authority has its office on Rhum and the 25 people living on the island are mostly employees of the Conservancy.

We had been late leaving Mallaig and we lost time on the journey round the islands, which was hardly surprising with the high seas running. But it was an exhilarating trip though I could imagine it becoming wearisome in the winter with no tourists or young people to enliven it.

Could it be boring, in spite of the grandeur of the scenery, operating these ferries, day after day and week after week? But one master assured me life on the ferry is never boring; no two journeys are alike, neither are the passengers who use the ferry. Officers and crew are a happy breed, courteous and polite and obviously content with their lot.

I have only mentioned about half of the ships in the Caledonian MacBrayne Fleet, but these, I hope, are indicative of the wide range of service offered by this well known Ferry Company. The ships on which I travelled are essentially ferries, though some also serve as cruise vessels when not required on ferry service.

The only other ferry company in this particular area is Western Ferries, who operate a small craft for passengers and cars from **McInroy's Point**, near Gourock, to **Hunter's Quay**, near Dunoon, and also from **Kennacraig**, the same terminal as Caledonian MacBrayne use at Kintyre, to **Port Askaig** on Islay.

Probably one of the best known ferries on the mainland was the **Ballachulish Ferry**, perhaps because of its association with the historical Glencoe area, but also because of the beauty of the scenery and its consequent popularity with the tourist population.

This ferry, like many others, saved the motorist about 20 miles when going south.

The Department of Trade, when making their Report on this ferry, pointed out that the ferry and the approaches to it formed a link between the Connel-Glencoe Trunk Road (A828) at North Ballachulish, in Argyllshire, and the Glasgow-Inverness Trunk Road (A82) at North Ballachulish, in Inverness-shire. They also stated that the ferry was, at the time (1948), in considerable demand by through traffic on the Glasgow-Inverness Trunk Road (A82) effecting a saving of about 12 miles compared with the alternative route through Kinlochleven. Vehicles were sometimes left waiting on the approaches and large vehicles, such as motor coaches, had to make the detour.

The D.o.T. Report therefore recommended that the ferry should be superseded by a bridge.

Commander I. T. Clark, late director of Ballachulish Ferry Company, was Manager for the Company from 1954 until it went into voluntary liquidation on 4th October 1975. He has given the following information. The first car was ferried in May 1906 on an open boat of about 14 feet in length, across which were placed two planks onto which the car was driven, as was the case with the Kyleakin Ferry in earlier times. The boat was propelled by sweeps (oars). With spring tide currents running at 7 knots through the strait, crossing was unlikely to have been made other than at or near slack water. The ferry is thought to have been mechanised about 1912. It was a motorboat carrying one car. Ballachulish Ferry Company was formed in 1935. Two-car boats, introduced about 1926, were considered adequate until 1951 when the increasing volume of traffic revealed the need for boats carrying four cars. Ferries were of wooden construction, built by James Noble & Son, of Fraserburgh, but the last, the *Glenachulish,* built by the Ailsa Shipbuilding Company of Troon, was of steel. All ferries had a turntable deck. The economic life of each boat was comparatively short due to strong tides, frequent high winds and quick turnover of traffic. Each boat crossed every seven minutes on average and all were powered by Gleniffer Diesel engines, apart from the last two which were fitted with Kelvin Diesel.

Vehicle charges were originally based on horse-power but later they were charged by the length of the vehicle and varied from 4s. 0d. to 6s. 0d., with 7s. 6d. for very large cars. Lorries were also charged by length. Fare boards showed all types of vehicles; bicycles, tandems, horse and cart, cows, stirks, sheep and foot passengers. Fares were originally collected on the ferry, but after a "man overboard" incident, when the day's takings were reputedly lost with the man, ticket-issuing kiosks came into operation. This was in 1955. Fares remained constant between 1954 and 1969 despite increased operating costs. Six houses free of rent and rates were provided for the coxswains. The increasing popularity of the ferry is evident by the fact that vehicular traffic increased from 42,000 in 1954 to 204,000 in 1974.

A letter sent to the officer stationed at Ballachulish on 12th February 1692, giving directions for putting into execution the service commanded against the rebels in Glencoe, had the following postscript: "Please order a guard to secure the ferry and the boats must all be on this syde of the Ferry after your men are over."

Car ferry crossing Loch Leven from North Ballachulish in 1975. *S. J. Boothman*

W. H. Murray's *Companion Guide to the West Highlands of Scotland* (1970 edition) draws attention to the fact that the Strait of Ballachulish is only 200 yards wide and "there has long been a demand for a bridge here, for long queues of cars form at both sides at the height of the summer."

Now at last there is a bridge and the ferry ceased to run on 4th October 1975.

Not far away the **Ardgour Ferry** still runs. It crosses the sea at Loch Linnhe linking the A872 in Inverness-shire with the A86 at Corran in Argyllshire. The A872 joins the Glasgow-Inverness Trunk Road (A82) at a point about 200 yards from the ferry. The only alternative route is by classified and trunk roads around Loch Linnhe and Loch Nil, the distance from terminal to terminal by this route being over 40 miles. The crossing, according to the Department of Trade Report, is the only direct means of access from the south to the large area enclosed by Loch Eil, Loch Linnhe, the Sound of Mull and Loch Shiel. The distance across the Corran Narrows is approximately 300 yards.

Peter MacQueen, Ferry Manager at Corran, in an interview with Joan Alison, said the first recorded date of the ferry is 1411, when the MacLeans of Ardgour took over the estate from the MacMasters. There was mention of a ferry in a book concerning the first battle of Inverlochy in 1431; also in a book entitled *Argyll and the '45.*

The first car crossed this ferry in 1934. The boat used was bought second-hand from the Ballachulish Ferry Company but the Company wished to keep the name *Glencoe* and the ferry boat was known at Corran as the *Tough*. It only carried one car at a time, the fare for cars being 10s. 0d. while passenger fare was 6d.

The next boat was built by Hendersons of Mallaig in 1939, and because of the war was not named until 1946 when she was called *North Argyll.* Powered by a 4-cylinder Kelvin Poppet engine of 26-30 h.p. she carried two cars. She was recorded as carrying a total of 19 cars on Easter Monday 1946.

Another 2-car boat was added in 1947, the *Maid of Glengour*. Increase in traffic necessitated the employment of two boats for the service; *Gorven*, carrying 4 cars and powered by a 4-cylinder, 48 h.p. Gardner engine, and the *Maid of Glengour* were the first boats built for the West Coast by James Noble of Fraserburgh.

For some reason, however, *Glengour* was sold and *Gorven* continued alone until joined by *Ben Kiel* in 1958. This was the first twin screw ferry to be used at Corran and carried five or six cars depending on their size. She was also built by James Noble. Another of his boats went into service at Corran in July 1964, the *Gleann Mhor.* It was intended that she should carry nine cars but this was found to be impracticable as it did not allow for egress from the vessel. The *Gorven* was sold later that year, and the *Ben Kiel* and *Gleann Mhor* continued in service until 1973 when *Lochaber*, which carried nine cars, arrived.

The ferry, which was leased to the Mackintosh family in 1936, was taken over by the Inverness County Council in November 1974 and by the Highland Regional Council in May 1975.

Qualifications to become a steersman include passing the test set by the Department of Trade and instituted in the 1960's, but anyone with four years service or more was automatically granted a Boatman's Licence and Passenger Certificate. This qualifies the holder to ferry 250 passengers, or the equivalent in passengers and cars. Questions are asked by the D.o.T. inspectors concerning International seamanship, systems of navigation, semaphore signals, fog signals, right of way, etc., but it is not necessary to have former seaman experience to join the ferry service. Most good ferrymen like to train their own crews.

Ferry boats in all parts of the country have to pass a D.o.T. test each year, to ensure that all aspects of the craft, including such things as engines and life saving and other equipment, reach the required standards.

At Corran there are six crew members and the manager, who work on a shift system, and from mid-June to September extra crew are taken on, these often being students.

There is a ferry across **Loch Cairnbawn to Kylestrome**, which runs seven days a week. The passage between the two promontories is little more than 300 yards and several islets protect it from the sea.

Local people will be glad to see a bridge over the Strait at this point. The distance across the ferry is 500 yards; the alternative route by road involves a detour of 100 miles.

Road widening from single track to two-way has been proceeding slowly on the Kylestrome shore of Loch Cairnbawn and the bridge is planned. It may be further west than the present terminal on the south side.

The ferry has been in the ownership of the Royal Automobile Club, the Filmer-Sankey family (Assynt Lodge) and Ronald Vestey. Following this the Sutherland County Council took over ownership and, in 1975, the Highland Regional Council took responsibility.

Interestingly the job of ferryman and of his wife as local school teacher are advertised together, with a house provided.

The *Maid of Glencoul*, the larger of the two boats operating on the **Kylesku-Kylestrome Ferry**, has two Caterpillar engines and a carrying limit of 35 tons. She is reversible and steered by the propellers and not a conventional rudder. The smaller vessel is the *Queen of Kylesku* which has two 110 h.p. Gardner engines and a carrying limit of 14 tons.

Coming up to Cape Wrath, on the northernmost tip of Western Scotland, there is no public highway in from the head of the Kyle of Durness but there is

Maid of Glencoul at Kylesku in 1977. *S. J. Boothman*

a roadway of the Northern Lighthouse Commission starting midway down the Kyle and winding ten miles over the moor of Parph to the Lighthouse. (Parph is a Gaelic rendering of the original Norse name for Cape Wrath—Hvarf, a turning point.)

The road can be reached by a passenger ferry from **Keoldale**. Until recently the only way was to walk to the Cape and back or hire a bicycle; an adventurous day's work in cold or windy weather and tough at the best of times.

I am indebted to Joan Alison, a journalist friend, who lives for part of the year in Sutherland, for much of the research of these ferries. She was talking to Hector MacKay, a seventy-nine year old man who was postman at **Durness** from 1949 to 1960. He told her his mother spoke of the ferry when he was a boy, so it must be over a hundred years old, as she remembered it all her life. The Campbells were the ferrymen at the beginning of the century but left in 1904. Angus Sutherland and his family moved into the ferryman's house on the west of the Kyle in 1904 and left in 1926 and a son of his took over the ferry for a year. From 1927-1936 Donald MacKenzie was ferryman; following him Donald Morrison operated it from 1936-1966. Oars and a sail had been the method of propulsion until Donald Morrison used an outboard motor. Charles Campbell was ferryman for a short time, followed by John Muir, who is currently operating the ferry, which belongs jointly to the Balnakiel Estate and the Scottish Lighthouse Commission. The ferry runs as required with no set time-table.

The Caledonian MacBrayne vessels *Loch Earn*, in foreground, and *Loch Nevis* in Tobermory Bay. *D. B. MacCulloch, Courtesy of the Oban Times*

A car and passenger service has been operating across the **Beauly Firth** between Inverness and the Black Isle. In the autumn of 1978, Joan Alison informs me that a bridge was being built across the Firth where the **Kessock Ferry** now runs. This is in accordance with the conclusion reached by the D.o.T. Committee's Report in 1948 which stated—"the existing facilities are inadequate to meet the present and future needs and a bridge will be required ultimately."

As a conclusion to this part of the Scottish Ferry story Joseph Mitchell has left on record a vivid description of the **Meikle Ferry** across the Dornoch Firth on the north eastern coast, as it existed in his father's days.

For three generations the ferry had been worked by a family of the name of Patience, whose mode of operation seems to have been singularly at variance with their name. The equipment of the ferry boat, according to Mitchell's description, left much to be desired. Broken ropes, torn sails and defective rudders appear to have been common occurrences, misfortunes less easily surmounted on the occasions when the thole pins, substitutes for row-locks, had been left behind. In John Mitchell's day there was no landing place on either side, while shallow water on the north side of the Firth meant that heavily laden boats must be off-shore until the tide was well in. Sometimes, in crossing to the north side, Mitchell had known the boat to be driven three or four miles up the Firth, waiting for the tide.

One of the worst accidents in the history of the Meikle Ferry took place in 1829. Only by the narrowest of margins did John Mitchell escape from being among the victims. Delayed in his journey from the south he reached the ferry to find, to his annoyance, that the boat had just left. The day was stormy, the boat heavily laden, and as he watched it, it was caught by the wind and overturned with the loss of a hundred lives. Had anything been needed to impress on John Mitchell the necessity and the urgency of the work of the Commissioners this must surely have supplied it.

Robert Southey reported, in 1819, that the Sutherland man who praised too highly Telford's bridge, and whose father had been one of the victims of the accident had been so shaken by what took place that, for ten years, he had preferred being cut off from the south side of the Firth to setting foot in a ferry boat. Perhaps Southey had the Meikle Ferry and its perils in mind when, later in his journey, he wrote of the Kessock Ferry over the Beauly Firth, which he had been assured was the best in Scotland, "but the best ferry is a bad thing."

But that was written a very long time ago and ferry boats are infinitely more reliable now.

CHAPTER SEVEN

Licenses and Tolls

IT IS interesting to examine some of the ancient leases granting the rights of ferries and to see exactly what the rights and duties of the lessees actually were. A good example is that relating to the Cremyll Ferry, as recorded by P. L. Hull in *The History of Cremyll Ferry*.

In the year 1588 Peter Edgcumbe held the exclusive right of this ferry and leased it first to Henry Blake at a rent of £6.10s.0d. per annum. Three years later it was leased to Peter, Henry's son, and his family. This lease included the passage house, the cottage and herbage and pasturing for one cow in the deer park until Peter could lease another place for pasturing a cow or two. With the ferry went the use of "the greate passinge boats" and the fees and profits, though, as was normally the case, Peter Edgcumbe and his family, servants and animals, had free passage. The lease passed down the family and eventually we find the Blake family holding the ferry from the time of the Armada (1588) almost to the outbreak of the Civil War (1642).

The terms imposed in the lease were that they were to "keep the passage house in repair and the great passinge boats and find sufficient men, boats and oars for the passage of people and with honest care and diligence to passe them over to and froe att all tymes convenyent and att prices accustomed and lawfull."

They were not to kill, embezzle, or take deer from the park at Mount Edgcumbe, and if they took any conies, "barbara hens", or pigeons from the park, or cut down oaks, ashes or elm trees there, they were to be liable to a fine of 40s. Also they were to keep their pigs in their outhouses and not to let them roam in the park. There were also many other matters covered in these ancient documents.

In 1639 the rent of the passage was still £6. 10s. 0d. but on 23rd March 1628 a down payment of £140 had been paid. Shortly afterwards, however, with the change in the lessee, the rent of the ferry was £4 a year plus £8. 10s. each lunar month for the fares. The passage house, stable and gardens and a palace were included! Two boats used for the passage, and an additional small boat, were to be kept in repair, the lessee also having to "trim and fitt them strong and staunch" every year and to provide enough men to work the ferry and to transport the mail or paquett. Cremyll carried the mail until Torpoint took it over in 1791.

There were occasions when the lessees' rights were taken away from them as in the case of the Saltash horse ferry boats. In 1804 the right to work the horse ferry boats at Saltash and receive tolls was let to the Saltash Corporation for £300 a year, but in 1832 an Act of Parliament took the rights away from the Corporation and gave them to a group of well-known people who established a steam ferry bridge with better accommodation and a consequent raising of tolls. However, seven years later, following litigation, the rights lapsed back to the Corporation.

In 1764, Mr Tucker, the landlord of the ferry house at Saltash, made it known that he had "lately fitted up his house, made a large stall, and provided everything good for the reception of travellers." He added:

> "Due attendance is given at the ferry and carriages safely put in and out of the ferry boat, the passage of which, for the encouragement of travellers, the Corporation have fixed at low rates:-
>
> A carriage and 6 7s. 6d.
> A carriage and 4 5s. 0d.
> A carriage and pair 2s. 6d.
> and one horse chaise 1s. 3d."

One of the duties of the Benedictines was to give hospitality to the wayfarer. Priories were, therefore, held responsible for the conduct of such ferries and dangerous fords.

Birkenhead was not a wealthy Priory and it was not long before the care of the passengers using the ferry became burdensome to the Prior and his brethren. Fog and storms were often responsible for several days delay to long distance travellers when the Priory was the only place where they could find food and lodging. Letters Patent were therefore granted to the Priory in 1317 giving permission to build a hostel for such people and to charge for hospitality to intending cross-river passengers detained by unfavourable weather.

In 1330 Edward III confirmed the Charter and the grants to the Prior and Convent of Birkenhead, and gave them "and their successors for ever" legal right of ferry to the Liverpool side "as well as for men as for horses and other things whatsoever," and the right to charge reasonable tolls for so doing.

Although provisions for hospitality for long distance travellers were made at priories and the numerous ferry inns throughout the country, there were abuses by some innkeepers responsible for the operation of the ferry, as we have seen earlier. Travellers also were warned about the over-charging of ferry fares. In 1797 for example, intending passengers on the Mersey were cautioned to make an agreement beforehand with the boatman, and not pay him until their return when a boat was hired especially to take them over. Otherwise, although on the regular ferry boats the charge was "twopence for market people and common passengers and sixpence is generally expected from the upper order of passengers, strangers were daily imposed upon, frequently to a shameful excess.*

In June 1824 fares seemed to change every week for the *Liverpool Mercury* advertised them as follows:-

11th June — 5d., 18th June — 3d., and 27th June — Free!

Payments in kind of one sort or another were prevalent on many ferries, and this applied also on sea ferries when there was keen competition to cover a profitable passage. In the case of some of the ancient river ferries this was written into the appropriate clause of the lease.

In 1839 the lessee of the Poole Ferry was entitled to 1d. per quarter from every householder and ½d. from every stranger. The collection from the householder was made quarterly through the town. The rent paid by John Hambury for the ferry and passage house was the annual provision of a couple of capons for the Mayor and his brethren.

The Deed of Conveyance for King's Lynn to West Lynn Ferry stipulated that John Ore, a burgess of Bishop's Lynn, should pay forty silver marks and a yearly rent of clove. When the ferry was taken over by the Corporation in 1649 it was let on a seven year lease to John Bird who agreed to pay £10 a year to the borough funds and make an annual present to the Mayor of a brace of well-fatted swans. The rent had risen to £200 a year by 1851, an indication of the popularity of the ferry which was a short cut to the Wash as well as useful to working people at West Lynn. There is no mention of swans or cloves being part of the rent at this time!

In the Charter granted to the Burgesses of Swansea in 1305 reference was made to the ferry which gave its name to Ferryside. Provision was made for a sheaf of wheat or 4d. per household to be exacted annually, which permitted people to use the Rivers Nedd and Tawe. This seems to be in addition to the toll charged for the actual voyage as these annual payments were set aside for the maintenance and support of the hospital, manor house and other institutions in the town.

In his *A Review of the Records of the Conway and Menai Ferries,* Henry Rees Davies writes of the disputes which arose concerning the leasing of the Conway Ferry to different people. In a case heard at the Sessions for the County of Caernarvon in 1395 he gives the rates of ferriage of that time as: "Taking of each man crossing alone — one farthing of fee. Of a man with a horse — one halfpenny. A man with a horse and with a load or any burden whatsoever, one penny . . . " Mr Davies states that this is the earliest record of ferry tolls at any of the North Wales ferries that has been found, and adds — "It is only incidentally, or in connection with disputes of one kind or another, that any mention of the charges made at the ferries has been met with prior to the

**The Rise and Progress of Wallasey* by E. C. Woods and F. C. Brown, Wallasey Corporation 1974.

19th century, and it is not until 1852 that we find an official schedule of the charges to be levied attached to a lease."

In 1688 a scale of charges was laid down for the Barton to Hull ferry which gave differing rates for "strangers", Freemen of Hull and inhabitants who were not Freemen.

When the fare across the Itchen Ferry was one penny, metal tokens were issued but after complaints by workers who had to cross the ferry twice daily, the fare was reduced to a halfpenny and new tokens had to be issued. These penny and halfpenny tokens were in use from 1865 to 1901 when they were discontinued. In 1961 a Fareham boy found one of the penny tokens clearly marked "Itchen Bridge 1d.", in his grandfather's garden.

Almost every village appears to have had its own market boat conveying villagers and their agricultural produce across the Humber, some making the journey twice a week, on Tuesday and Thursday market days, while others made less frequent visits.

These were not in competition with the ferries, but lessees jealously guarded their rights. These market boats helped to create congestion along the waterfront at Hull, making disembarking hazardous and uncomfortable. Ferry passengers often had to use a small boat to land or cross several vessels before they could reach the landing place.

Actual opposition, however, came from James Acland who, not being a native of Hull, claimed that tolls were illegally high. In 1831 he toured the bridges refusing to pay tolls. So great was the excitement he created that it is claimed a thousand special constables had to be sworn in to preserve the peace. He turned his attention to the ferries, quoting the charter granted by King Edward five centuries earlier, which fixed the rate at a halfpenny. Acland urged the people to insist on their rights and refuse to pay more. When the ferryman declined to accept these lower fees Acland set up his own boat—the *Public Opinion*. Although smaller and inferior to the ferry it was popular and the ferry lost many of its passengers. However, Acland soon found it necessary to charge more than a halfpenny though he continued to undercut the ferry. In spite of this he lost money on the venture and had to give up, but not before rivalry occurred between the *Public Opinion* and the ferry boat, *Royal Charter,* with both boats racing across the Estuary with resultant bumpings and collisions.

Eventually the Corporation brought an action against him and when the trial was over his popularity had waned. He was forced to raise the toll on his boat to sixpence and then to withdraw the *Public Opinion* in disrepair.

Ferries served all kinds of purposes. A story of the Sussex scene in bygone days is mentioned in an article in *Sussex Life*. It concerns a ferry, known as the Old Corpse Ferry on which, after the last rites for the dead had been performed in Appledram Church, in the Chichester area, the bodies of parishioners were ferried through the winding water channels on their final journey to interment at Bosham.

Cremyll and Torpoint ferries each had a stated charge for transporting a hearse. The fares on the Cremyll/Stonehouse Ferry in 1742 were—for a hearse without the coffin 10s. 6d., with the coffin one guinea. Torpoint, however, obviously assumed they would not be required to convey hearse and coffin both ways for their fee was for every hearse going with and returning the same day without a corpse, 10s. 6d.! This ferry also included in the same set of fees the rate for a dog going and returning once in the same day, including the person attending, 2d. Few other accounts of ferries mention dogs. Torpoint seemed to be more explicit in publicising their tolls for also included in the list is a toll of 6d. for every ton of goods of any kind of merchandise and for every hogshead of beer or other liquor a toll of 6d.

Kylesku Ferry indicating charges in 1977. *S. J. Boothman*

CHAPTER EIGHT

Ferrymen

"Of all the mortals here below
Your drunken boatmen are the worst I know
I'm here determined, though against my will
While these and fellows sit and drink their fill,
Oh Jove! to my request let this decree
That these same boatmen ne'er see hell nor heaven
But with old Charon ever tug the oar
And neither taste nor swallow one drop more."

SO, IT is reported, wrote an impatient farmer in September 1891 concerning the fickle ferrymen and boatmen concerned with the Helford River Passage at that time.

There is a story that, a few years earlier, a certain Miss Fox, disgusted at the tolls imposed by these "indolent boatmen" on those going to market in Falmouth, had a wooden house built on the Lizard side so that intending passengers would at least wait in shelter rather than be forced to walk round by way of Gweek or spend their time and money in the public house. True, this lady did have the wooden shelter erected. The reason attributed for it had not been proved but there were many complaints about ferrymen in various places in earlier times.

During the closing years of the eighteenth century the delays of the boatmen and the treatment of animals were causes of censure. One traveller records that "besides the inconvenience naturally attending us wading a stream in a place subject to all the variants produced by the flowing and ebbing of tides that run sometimes very high, most of the travellers who have crossed here (except the passengers in the mail coach, who, by order of the Post Office, have a boat always waiting for them) know what it is to experience wilful delays and grossest and bare-faced impositions of the ferrymen, with regard to charges."*

Weather one could not control, and this included the Severn Bore, but the boatmen were often callous and careless; to them another life or two lost by drowning sometimes appeared to be of little account.

***A Review of the Records of the Conway and the Menai Ferries.* University of Wales Press Board, 1966.

Inns were built on both sides of the river for the benefit of travellers using the passages over the Severn. Between the seventeenth and eighteenth centuries innkeepers operated the ferry. All seemed well until the early years of the nineteenth century when there were complaints that these landlords purposely delayed the departure of the ferry so that passengers were obliged to remain at the inn overnight. In 1828, with the appointment of a respectable superintendent to manage the ferries, the landlords became more civil.

Extracts from the Court Rolls of South Shields, in the sixteenth and seventeenth centuries, relating to the Shields ferryboats stipulate that, if:

> "farmers or occupiers of ye said boates from time to time doe not, when passengers come to the waterside for passing and repassing ouer the water, thoroughly convey them ouer, that then for every neglect or refusal the said farmer or farmers or occupiers of the ferry boates shall pay to the lords of the manor 12d.
> And that the horse boates bee from time to time moored in some convenient place into the low water marke or as neare as conveniently may bee, whereby the said boates may be in readiness to carry or take horses, beasts or other goodes ouer the water, or else farmers or occupiers shall pay for every neglect 2d."

The Conway was a particularly difficult crossing, partly because of the quicksands and partly because of the delays and behaviour of the ferrymen at one time, some of whom seem to have had an especially bad reputation. One traveller who was touring Wales on horseback with a friend, in July 1784, tells how their horses were obliged to leap into and out of deep water adding:

> "My horse performs these operations awkwardly and Mr P's would not enter for ten minutes! Another tourist says that he was much annoyed at the way in which his horses were flogged into the ferry boat, but he 'might as well have addressed the boat as the boatmen'."

An incident published in the *North Wales Gazette* in 1808 states that at six o'clock in the evening the horse boat sailed from the Denbighshire side of the river with the goods of the Chester waggon.

> "There were on board Mr Williams, the Proprietor of the waggon, Mr Samuel Walker of Beaumaris, with his horse and the three ferrymen. There was a heavy storm and in the darkness the boatmen lost their bearings but by good fortune reached an island. Here the ferrymen, on the pretence of calling for help, left the boat. The horse was got out but the boat sank and the goods were lost, despite Mr Williams' attempt to save them. Volunteers from Conway eventually rescued the party."

The report ends:

> "No comments are necessary on the conduct of the boatmen, it being universally allowed that the Conway boatmen are, in general, far more disagreeable to passengers than the ferry itself."

There is an apocryphal story concerning the Topsham Ferry. A group of students one evening hailed the ferryman five minutes after the last ferry was due to have run. He rowed out to within a few yards of the bank and told them the last ferry had gone. Then he rowed back—without them!

This ferry was out of action a number of times due to the difficulty of finding ferrymen to operate it. In 1960 it was reported that a man who accepted the position at a salary of £300 a year, plus fees, then asked that the fee which, for years, had been 2d., should be increased. As a result the ferry was closed for six months during which time the fourteen-year-old son of the lock-keeper was unable to cross the Exe to catch his train to school.

Still ferrymen came and went, with the ferry frequently temporarily out of action in consequence, causing considerable hardship and frustration. In 1968 a salary of £350 a year and the proceeds of the fees was offered, but the ferryman would have to provide his own boat. At that time the fees were 4d. and the ferry was operating from 8 o'clock to 5.30 from October to April and 7.30 to 10 at night during the summer months. By 1974 the ferryman's salary had been increased to £12 for a 66½ hour week in winter and an 84 hour week in summer, and he kept the fees—4p per person, 2p for a dog and 3p for a cycle. But the ferry has since been closed.

The more usual pattern, however, was that the ferryman's job was passed from father to son and remained in the same family for many years, and most were much more honest and reliable than the verse quoted at the beginning of this section, and the incidents recorded, seem to indicate. Indeed, there are plenty of examples of devotion to duty, sometimes to the extent of ferrymen losing their lives in the process.

An unusual accident was "engineered" by the ferrymen at the New Passage from Chessel Pil to Portskewett following the escape of Charles I from the Roundheads. Although he and his party were ferried safely over, the Roundheads were so hotly in pursuit that they were at the ferry demanding to be taken over almost as soon as the boats had returned. When the ferrymen at first refused they were forced into their boats at the point of a sword. Having no alternative but to obey the ferrymen rowed them over to the place known as the English Stones, where, at low tide, passengers could walk to the Gloucestershire side of the river. There the ferrymen disembarked their passengers knowing that their enemies were quite unaware that the tide was on the turn and there was no time to reach the other shore before being engulfed by the river. All sixty Roundheads were drowned.

The Brotherhood of Ferrymen, like the ferries they operate, are of an infinite variety. Some wear civilian clothes like the old ferryman who rowed the Deben at Woodbridge whilst others served in uniform such as these Mersey ferrymen with their powered craft.

R. Edwards in JV-R Collection *Bob Bird of Wallasey*

The operation of the ferry from Itchen to Southampton was the responsibility of the Geary family for almost ninety years. Grandfather Geary had been a boatman for sixteen years, from 1864 when he took people over in a rowing boat. His second son served as bridgeman and assistant superintendent for more than thirteen years before leaving for Australia. A younger son was then engaged as bridgeman and toll collector and served for thirty years when ill-health forced him to retire. He, in turn, was followed by his son, who served first on the Floating Bridge and then as toll collector.

At Wick Ferry I was told of another family who had kept the ferry going from 1800 until 1903, when Mr Edmunds appears to have purchased it and continued to own it until he retired in 1946. In his early years work began at 5.30 in the morning and finished at 11 o'clock at night. Mr O'Brien, whose portrait appeared in the Royal Academy, helped operate the ferry. He was described as "a huge man, so big his sister had to make special boots for him."

Edmunds is credited with having built the boathouse on the Christchurch side in 1927 and started a caravan camp which he sold when he retired from the ferry service.

One instance revealing how keen this ferryman was to keep the ferry working no matter what the conditions is the action he took in 1934 when he found the ferry iced over, the first time this had happened for a hundred years. The boatman cut a channel enabling him to operate, but in the afternoon the floating ice collected more quickly than he could clear it so that he was unable to move in either direction. Men were sent out from the holiday camp which, by that time had taken over the ferry, and after an hour the boatman was freed. Meantime the ferry operated as usual through another channel.

Hayle Ferry, in Cornwall, is a classic example of one which has been operated by men who have spent most of their lives on it.

In his book, *Beloved St Ives,* Cyril Noall talks of an aged Lelant native who wrote, in 1935, of Tom Gale, who held the office of ferryman for a period of forty years around the middle of the nineteenth century.

> "Maybe there are many yet who have heard of, if not personally known, the old ferryman who paddled his old flat-bottomed praam across the Hayle River from Lelant Towans to the beach on the Phillack side, fifty, sixty and I expect seventy years ago. How well do I remember, on Whit-Mondays, when there was a gala on the Phillack Towans or a regatta at the Copperhouse Pool, there would be scores of people returning to the Leland side and, if the tide had turned to go out, and a strong current was pouring out from Lelant mud, the ferryman and his praam would be swept down the stream as if t'were but a straw. Notwithstanding this, not even the most ardent lovers from St Ives would think of going round via the Causeway, but, braving the terrors of the deep, would

> cross in the ferryboat, and then meander up the Church Lane, and on through Longstone, Chyangwheal and Trelyon."

Noall goes on to relate that a relative, Thomas Whatty the elder, followed Tom Gale as ferryman but about 1889 his term of service finished in tragedy.

> "Late one evening, after Whatty had ceased work for the day, two men hailed him and asked to be conveyed to the Hayle shore. Tom Whatty was most reluctant to accede to their request because of the darkness and the strong current then running, but at last he allowed himself to be persuaded—against his better judgement—to take the men across. None of them survived the journey, and as there were no witnesses to the accident which overwhelmed the boat, it will never be known precisely how the three men met their deaths. Only one body—that of one of the passengers—was recovered. Tom Whatty himself was a strong swimmer and should have experienced no difficulty reaching the shore after the ferry had capsized. It must be assumed, therefore, that he lost his life in attempting to save one of the passengers, being seized in a death-grip by the drowning man, and so dragged down with him to a watery grave. The missing bodies were either swept to sea or, more probably, buried in the sand and silt of the river."

But this did not deter his son, Thomas Whatty the younger, from succeeding him. In all, four successive members of the same family operated this ferry.

One day a so-called "sportsman", armed with a gun, arrived at the river intent of shooting birds. Whilst crossing the ferry Whatty attracted his passenger's attention to their strange companion, remarking, "My baby seal is just behind you, coming after us."

The sportsman instantly whipped up his gun, pressed the trigger, and scattered the brains of the too-trusting seal over the surface of the water.

This younger Whatty was one of the most popular ferrymen Lelant has ever known. He did not live to a great age and was followed by his son, the fourth successive member of the same family to hold the appointment.

Another ferry which was served by one family for a long period was the White Rock Ferry which was taken over by the Swansea Corporation in 1939. By that time it had been in the ownership of the Clarke family for fifty-four years. It was closed in 1945.

When I crossed on the Bawdsey Ferry with Charlie Brinkley he told me he had been running this ferry for seventeen years. His last boat was launched in 1973 and he said it had earned its keep by ferrying R.A.F. men across to their Station. He was working 78 hours during a seven-day week including Christmas Day and Boxing Day. There were not many civilian passengers but the R.A.F. needed a ferry from 6.50 a.m. until 11.15 p.m. and he could not find anyone to help him out. But with the closure of the Camp early in 1977, and the consequent loss of the contract coupled with diminished ordinary traffic on the ferry, Charlie Brinkley has been losing money.

This is yet another instance of long serving ferrymen in one family for Charlie's father operated the ferry from 1895-1939. Charlie was born in one of the cottages built by the Quilter family who owned the ferry when Charlie's father was operating the chain ferry. He retired when the vehicular service was withdrawn.

In 1975, when efforts were being made to obtain a subsidy to keep the ferry operating, a member of the Felixstowe Preservation Society wrote: "Charlie Brinkley is running his ferry at the moment because he won't let people down. He regards his passengers as his friends and it is costing him money."

A few months before I met him Charlie had received a signal honour. The Central Board of the R.A.F. and a Guard of Honour from R.A.F. Bawdsey were present when Charlie Brinkley received the British Empire Medal for "outstanding service" to the R.A.F. in his work as ferryman. The award was presented by Air Vice Marshal Ivor Brown.

Another outstanding figure in the ferry scene is Enoch Williams, of Chepstow. I was unable to meet him when I was in the area, but I heard quite a lot about him from the three retired ferrymen whom I did meet and I had a brief telephone conversation with his son John, who worked with his father after he returned from Army service.

Swansea-born Enoch Williams, who was in the Royal Engineers in the First World War, received no medal but when the Severn Bridge was opened in 1966 he received £90,000 in compensation for the closing of the Aust/ Beachley Ferry.

After negotiating the rights with the Duke of Beaufort, whose family owned them, Enoch Williams had set about reviving this ancient ferry nearly forty years after it had lapsed when the Severn Railway Tunnel undermined its usefulness. He began by borrowing a motor boat from a friend at Barry to run groceries and provisions between South Wales and the West Country. The passenger fare was 1s. 0d. and it remained so for the forty-five years during which he owned it. By the early 1930s he had formed, with some friends, the Old Passage Severn Ferry Company and had purchased the first vehicle ferry, the *Princess Ida*, named after his wife, and begun regular services. He did not operate the boats himself, but in bad weather he made the crossing with the passengers, saying it gave them confidence if the boss was aboard. The latter years of the 1930s were the best, he recalled. Profits were good, taxation low, trade was growing, men were easy to get and there were no long queues of frustrated motorists waiting to cross.

The Beachley/Aust ferry made Enoch a modest fortune but it gave him something else—contentment. He says: "You know, building up the ferry business has been the happiest time of my life, it was building something that no-one else had the guts to do. They were afraid of the tides, but if people had been able to cross with sailing boats I reckoned that it could be done without too much difficulty with motor boats!"

It should also be added that he had some very good men working the ferries.

There was Ben Brown, who had been skipper of the *Severn Queen* ferrying across the Severn from 1952 until the ferry closed in 1966, telling me the tide sometimes made it necessary to make twenty manoeuvres to get her alongside. They had to edge across crabwise in these flat-bottomed boats with no keel, drawing less than five feet of water. He spoke of the time when two tankers collided, blowing up the bridge which was being built, with the loss of five lives. He introduced me to Captain Groves who, at eighteen years of age, was master of a sailing boat and who was ferrying at Beachley for twenty-five years and now long since retired.

Then there was Percy Palmer, the longest serving member of this ferry. His wife is a town councillor. He started as deck hand on the old *Princess Ida*. On one occasion, when he was deck hand on the *Severn King* the skipper failed to turn up. Percy waited for ten minutes then took the boat out himself; his first experience as skipper. He became permanent skipper of the *Severn King*, then of the *Severn Queen*. He served on the ferries for thirty-one years and in that time made 200,000 to 220,000 trips. It was he who made the last trip as ferry master on the day the bridge was opened.

He spoke of the passengers he had taken across, among them Queen Mary and Amy Johnson, from whom he has a letter of thanks for his help when she ran out of petrol. "She wasn't in a plane then," he says, "but in a car."

It was at 6 o'clock on the 8th September 1966 that he took the *Severn Princess* on her last official trip across the river. All the ferries were dressed overall with signal flags from masthead to wheelhouse and the Red Ensign was flown aft. The Union Jack and the Welsh National Flag were flown at both Beachley and Aust Piers.

The next day Percy Palmer became inspector of toll keepers on the new bridge which had been opened by the Queen, working above the river instead of on it.

Some ferries are remembered more by the name of the ferrymen than by the places from which they operate. Pull's Ferry, once called Sandlin's Ferry, close by the old city gate in Norwich, is one such. Sandlin was said to be a chorister in the reign of Elizabeth I. A Norwich directory of 1841 refers to "Sandlin's Ferry, so called from one of the name by whom it was formerly kept, is situated on the east side of the precinct, and has been used as a ferry from time immemorial. There was a double arch of black flint with a residence for the keeper who was responsible to the Dean."

John Pull, according to the Chapter Book, was admitted to the office of Keeper of the Ferry in 1796 and was both ferryman and publican. Pull was described as a "kind old fellow, dressed all in black, with a white frilled shirt, and a long white neck scarf which was wound about his neck two or three times."

During the time he lived at the Ferry House, in the latter years of the eighteenth and the early nineteenth centuries, the Apollo Band practised there. On Thursday afternoons in the summer the musicians floated along the river in a barge, the *Apollo*, playing upon their wind instruments. The band was "a source of much gratification to its numerous visitors, and the attendant parties who followed in other boats to listen to the music." The owner of the *Apollo* was Daniel Clarke, known as "The Admiral of the Flotilla." He died in 1827 at the age of eighty-two.

Dant's Ferry, Cambridge, is another of the ferries known better by the name of its ferrymen than by the name of the ferry, the Cutter Ferry, so named from the *Cutter Inn* which once stood immediately against it on the Chesterton side of the ferry.

The Dant family owned the ferry for many years. In May 1893, after the death of David Dant, the elder, the ferry was auctioned with its adjacent land.

Dants had been watermen from the early 1700s and they had many ties by marriage with other families engaged in the Fenland trade. David Dant, the first owner, was the sixth in direct descent from John Daunte of St Ives, who was born in 1630.

Today many mourn the passing of river ferries as they give place to bridges which take the traveller over rather than on the river. While this may be easier and quicker than the old way, and we may often have reason to be grateful, much of the pleasure and more leisurely appreciation of the journey has gone. Where we once had to queue to cross the river, we now travel at ever increasing speed along our by-passes and motorways, getting more and more frustrated when traffic builds up to cause us delay. It is the price of progress, but I often want to echo the couplet written by William Henry Davies—

"What is this life if, full of care,
We have no time to stand and stare?"

Long live the river ferries.

Bibliography

Allison, J. E., *The Mersey Estuary.* David & Charles.
Brown, Lilian, *All about Bury.* Combridge House, 1948.
Davies, Henry Rees. *A Review of the Records of the Conway and the Menai Ferries.* University of Wales Press Board, 1966.
Defoe, Daniel, *Tour Through England and Wales.* 1724.
D'Orley, Alan A., *The Humber Ferries.* Nidd Valley Narrow Gauge Railways Ltd. 1968
Duckham, Baron F., *The Yorkshire Ouse.* 1967.
Duckworth and Langmuir, *West Coast Steamers.* T. Stephenson, 1967.
Duckworth and Langmuir, *West Highland Steamers.* T. Stephenson, 1968.
Farr, Grahame, *Chepstow Ships.* The Chepstow Society and the Newport and Monmouth Branch of the Historical Society.
Farr, Grahame, *West Country Passenger Steamers.* T. Stephenson, 1967, 2nd edition.
Fiennes, Celia, *Through England on a Side-Saddle in the time of William and Mary 1695/97.*
Gilpin, William, *Observations on the River Wye, 1782 and 1789.*
Henderson, Charles, *Essays on Cornish History.* Oxford University Press, 1936.
Hodgson, George B., *The Borough of South Shields from the Earliest Period to the Close of the Nineteenth Century.* 1977.
Hoskins, W. G., *Devon — A New Survey of England, 1954.* 1st impression.
Hull, P. L., *History of Cremyll Ferry before 1230.*
Jordan, Christopher, *Severn Enterprise.* Arthur Stockwell, 1977.
Lindsey, *Season at Harwich.* 1851.
Malster, Robert, *Wherries and Waterways,* Terence Dalton, 1971.
McCrorie, Ian, *Ships of the Fleet.* Caledonian MacBrayne, 1977.
Morgan, Cliff, *Briton Ferry (Llansawel).* Cliff Morgan, 1977.
Mould, George, *Lancashire's Unknown River.* Terence Dalton, 1970.
Mudie, *History of Hampshire.* 1838.
Murray, W. H., *Companion Guide to the West Highlands of Scotland.* Collins, 1970.
Noall, Cyril, *Beloved St. Ives.* Bradford Barton, 1958.
Pannell, P. M., *Old Southampton Shores.* David & Charles, 1967.
Paterson, Alan, *The Golden Years of the Clyde Steamers.* David & Charles, 1969.
Paterson, Alan, *Victorian Summer of the Clyde Steamers.* David & Charles, 1973.
Perry, John, *American Ferryboats.* 1957.
Pudney, John, *Crossing London's River.* Dent, 1972.
Redstone, Lilian, *Bygone Woodbridge.*
Seymour, J., *Companion Guide to East Anglia.* Collins, 1970.
Swire, Otta F., *Skye — The Island and its Legends.* Blackie, 1961.
Vosper, Douglas C., *The Ancient Ferry at Saltash.*
Webb, William (Editor), *Memorials of Exmouth.* 1872.
Wesley, John, his *Journal.*
Wood, G. Bernard, *Ferries and Ferrymen.* Cassells, 1969.
Woods, E. C. and Brown, P. C., *The Rise and Progress of Wallasey,* Wallasey Corporation. 1929 1st ed. (1974 edition used in research).
Woods, E. Cuthbert and Jones, E., *Some History of the Wallasey Luggage Boats from 1st April 1880 to 31st March 1947.* Transactions of the Liverpool Nautical Research Society, Vol. X, 1961-71.
Department of Trade — Report, 1949.

Index

INDEX